MW00777719

UNDERTORAH:
AN EARTH-BASED KABBALAH OF DREAMS

"Jill Hammer is one of the most original thinkers in contemporary spirituality, and this book is her most original yet. *Undertorah* is a passionate call to reimagine the role of dreams in our daily lives, and in the process, find a way to both deepen our connection to the planet and enrich our understanding of ourselves. A wonderful achievement."

> —**Bruce Feiler**, *New York Times* bestselling author of *Walking the Bible* and *Life Is in the Transitions*

"*Undertorah* is a dream book for our time and beyond. Rabbi Hammer reveals how dreams can grant us healing access to the world of the sacred, not only in our personal lives but in 'our collective journey as a species and an ecosystem.' I have been inspired by Rabbi Jill Hammer's amazing gifts as a storyteller, a student and teacher of Talmud and kabbalah, a visionary, a poet, and above all a woman for whom the complex realities of our minds and spirits, our living earth, and the vast cosmos, are linked—ultimately—by love. Here is a book that will change the lives of all who read it."

> —**Dr. Alicia Ostriker**, author of *The Volcano and After: Selected and New Poems 2002–2019,* Chancellor of the Academy of American Poets (2015–2020), and New York State Poet Laureate (2018–2021)

"Like Nobel-prize winner Tomas Tranströmer, Rabbi Jill Hammer is a down-to-earth mystic who lives and writes at the intersection of dreaming and waking, vision and reality, individuality and Oneness, everyday existence and revelation. Reading dreams with the depth and precision with which poets read poems and geographers read maps, this book opens doors between realms and teaches us to follow our dreams through them, guiding us from 'fear, resentment, inhibition, apathy, and regret' to the place within each of us where we 'can meet the cosmos that lies beyond our limited consciousness.'"

—**Dr. Joy Ladin**, award-winning poet and author of *The Future is Trying to Tell Us Something* and *Through the Door of Life*

"Jill Hammer's *Undertorah* thoroughly persuades me that when we honor our dreams and treat them as sacred forms of communication, they can be powerful sources of wisdom, connection, and healing. Like any other spiritual discipline, reading one's dreams takes diligent attention and skill, and this rich book offers traditional Jewish and contemporary techniques for dreaming productively—calling us to experience dreams as meaningful gifts with truly transformative potential."

—**Dr. Vanessa Ochs**, author of *The Jewish Dream Book* and *Inventing Jewish Ritual*

"Rabbi Hammer has opened for us a portal to the dreamworld, a place that holds the beauty and power we need to meet the challenges of our time. Drawing on both the vast treasures of ancient wisdom, and the courage and creativity of a living community of seekers, she guides us toward a meeting with the Great Mystery: where we can be called to awareness and loving communion with the One. *Undertorah* is an important book for the healing of our individual stories and for the healing of the world we share."

—**Rabbi Shefa Gold**, author of *The Magic of Hebrew Chant: Healing the Spirit, Transforming the Mind, Deepening Love* and *Are We There Yet? Travel as a Spiritual Practice*

"*Undertorah* uniquely positions dreams as 'poems we and the Divine send one another.' Rabbi Hammer deftly illustrates how dreams 'whisper in fragmented images, like a mosaic' of a Presence that 'infuses the universe with life and meaning.' Every dream, Hammer tells us, is a potential portal to the Presence underlying and animating our life and world. With lucid language and gentle guidance, she masterfully leads us into the depths of our imagination—empowering us to experience the joy, enchantment, and enlightenment dreams can offer."

—**Catherine Shainberg, PhD**, author of *Kabbalah and the Power of Dreaming, DreamBirth: Transforming the Journey of Childbirth through Imagery,* and the forthcoming book, *The Kabbalah of Light*

"*Undertorah* is a book that redeems our dreams, gently shifting awareness away from the harsh spotlight of personal psychology, and into the dark, mysterious and permeable underworld of memory, earth, presence, and revelation. Rabbi Jill Hammer's new book is a cairn on the journey of understanding and repair—a kaleidoscopic collection of story, text, recollection, and wisdom. This indispensable work creatively interprets the subterranean messages of element, animal, ancestor, and divine feminine, offering us a holistic way to transform and heal from the gift of our dreams."

—**Day Schildkret**, author of *Hello, Goodbye: 75 Rituals for Times of Loss, Celebration, and Change* and *Morning Altars: A 7-Step Practice to Nourish Your Spirit through Nature, Art, and Ritual*

"Rabbi Jill Hammer has uncovered the soul of our dreaming, that numinous place of learning, experience, and divine wisdom that takes us far beyond the dry symbology of twentieth-century thinking. As we teeter on the brink of extinction, we need to find authentic ways to connect to the Web of Life in all its forms, so that we and the living world might move forward together. Jill Hammer's *Undertorah* is the tool kit for the new millennium, brought to us in ways that are articulate, grounded, magical and—crucially—accessible to everyone."

—**Manda Scott**, *Sunday Times* bestselling author of *Boudica: Dreaming the Eagle* and cofounder of the *Accidental Gods* podcast

This book was made possible through the
generous support of the Opaline Fund.
We are grateful for their commitment to
the transformative power of creative work,
and to amplifying a polyphony of voices
from within and beyond the Jewish world.

Cover design, book design, and typesetting by
Becca Lofchie

Cover photograph by Sam Haddix

Ayin Press
Brooklyn, New York
www.ayinpress.org
info@ayinpress.org

Distributed by Small Press Distribution

Printed in the United States of America

ISBN: 978-1-5323-6200-2

Library of Congress Control Number:
2021947462

Ayin Press books may be purchased
at a discounted rate by book clubs,
synagogues, and other institutions
buying in bulk. For more information,
please email info@ayinpress.org.

Undertorah:
An
Earth-Based
Kabbalah of
Dreams

Jill
Hammer

AYIN PRESS XXXX

Dedicated to Raya Leela Jedwab-Hammer,
my deep-dreaming daughter,

to Shoshana Jedwab,
with whom I share waking and dreaming,

and to Leonard Hammer, my father, of blessed memory—
may he always visit my dreams.

Contents

ACKNOWLEDGMENTS

This book could not have been written without all the dreamers I interviewed and counseled, or without the dreamers who wrote about their dreams in books and articles. I am especially grateful to them for their vision, vulnerability, and generosity of spirit. Gratitude also to scholars and workers of dreams from antiquity to the present, from whose wisdom I constantly benefit.

Special thanks go to the dreamers of the Kohenet Hebrew Priestess Institute and the dreamers of the Academy for Jewish Religion—our journeys through the dreamworld have changed my life. I also thank all the dreamers in dream circles I have attended or facilitated—Romemu, ALEPH, my online classes, and other places—you have added much to my understanding!

Deepest gratitude goes to Eden Pearlstein, Kristin Nelson, Tom Haviv, Becca Lofchie, Penina Eilberg-Schwartz, Joanna Steinhardt, and to everyone at Ayin Press who skillfully and patiently helped birth this book into being. Thank you all for bringing this dream to life. Thanks also to Sam Haddix for the cover photo, to Kohenet Annabel Cohen for Yiddish translation help, and to Dr. Devin Naar for help with Ladino transliteration. I am so profoundly grateful to Kohenet Renee Finkelstein, editor extraordinaire, for finding the threads of light in this book and helping to weave them into a meaningful pattern.

I also wish to thank dreamworkers Dr. Catherine Shainberg and Rodger Kamenetz, teachers from whom I have learned so much, as well as dreamworkers Mary Jo Heyen and Kezia Vida, who have also been of great service to me. And much gratitude to others who have advised me and supported the book: Rav Kohenet Taya Mâ Shere, Rhonda Rosenheck, Rabbi Amichai Lau-Lavie, Manda Scott, Dr. Alicia Ostriker, Dr. Nathaniel Berman, Dr. Joy Ladin, Dr. Elizabeth Denlinger, Bruce Feiler, Dr. Vanessa Ochs, Rabbi Arthur Waskow, Rabbi Shefa Gold, and Day Schildkret.

I am so deeply grateful to my wife Shoshana and daughter Raya, who have generously supported this work and who are always part of my waking and dreaming worlds. I remember with love my father Leonard Hammer, of blessed memory, who shared his dreams with me. I am grateful to my mother Erna Hammer and the rest of my family for their understanding as I created this book (and relentlessly asked them about their dreams!). I offer profound gratitude to the Source of Dreams, and to the dreamworld that has guided me throughout my life and brought me to this moment.

A NOTE ON THE
DREAMERS

In this book, I have included dreams from ancient, medieval, and modern texts as well as contemporary sources such as books, articles, websites, and interviews. Additionally, I myself have interviewed many dreamers during this process. Some I have worked with as a dreamworker, and some I interviewed regarding a particular dream or dreams. I interviewed people from many walks of life: rabbis, cantors, kohanot (ordinees of the Kohenet Hebrew Priestess Institute), chaplains, ministers, divinity students, psychotherapists, physicians, computer programmers, musicians, incarcerated people, academics, media workers, childcare workers, retirees, artists, and activists. The dreamers I have interviewed for the chapters of this book have generously volunteered to offer these evocative, vulnerable recollections of their intimate dream processes. I am grateful to them for their willingness, their courage, and their thoughtfulness. Without their dreams, I would not have been able to develop the ideas and practices presented in this book.

I interviewed sixty-eight dreamers for the book, and of those, thirty-five dreamers appear in these pages. The dreamers included in this book come from the United States, Canada, Great Britain, Germany, and Spain. The dreamers represented in the book are of many ages, genders, sexual orientations, and racial backgrounds; a majority of them are women. Most of the dreamers I interviewed and included in the book are Jewish; about a sixth are of other traditions or backgrounds. The dreamers appear pseudonymously in order to protect their privacy.

Throughout the book, I have offered my understanding of these dreamers' dreams. Of course, no dream should be limited to a single interpretation, and I have not in any way exhausted the possible meanings of each dream. I have tried as much as possible to correct my own understanding by asking the dreamers what they feel and observe about their own dreams.

I am profoundly grateful to all the dreamers for the visions they have shared. I hope they will inspire readers to find the power and healing in their own dreams.

Where the wilderness enters, the world, the
    song of the world ...
This night. The way in.
        —Muriel Rukeyser, "Akiba"

A dream is a scripture, and many scriptures
are nothing but dreams.
        —Umberto Eco, *The Name of the Rose*

Undertorah: An Earth-Based Kabbalah of Dreams

It happened like this: one day, a friend told me she'd had a dream about me. That wasn't so unusual on its own. But that same day, I heard from another friend who had also had a dream about me. And then, in the days that followed, a total of ten people contacted me to tell me I had been in their dream. No one had dreamt the same dream—they'd all been different, but it was the number that struck me.

Nonplussed, I asked a few of my wisest teachers what they thought this might mean. None of them had an answer for me. "But it must mean *something!*" I thought. I concluded that I was receiving an invitation from the dreamworld. I decided then to delve into its mysteries and see what happened. I'd always paid attention to my dreams, but now I began to study them in earnest.

I read books on dreaming. I pored over biblical passages that described prophetic dreams and explored the Talmud's mysterious section on dream interpretation. I learned about the women and men of sixteenth-century Tzfat, who understood their dreams as a source of soul-knowledge. I taught classes on Jewish dreaming, and studied with Jewish dreamworkers.

Over the years, my dream journeys helped me change professions, heal my illnesses, cope with motherhood, and face my father's death. I began to understand dreaming as a pilgrimage: a journey to a mysterious, magical place where strange beings, places, and stories revealed hidden truths. Dreams were a labyrinth I walked nightly, a labyrinth whose twists and turns I could sometimes remember.

But this labyrinth didn't end when I awoke. As I deepened my dream practice, I realized that at least half of the journey occurred once I reentered the waking world. Writing down the dream, sharing it with others, listening to their responses, receiving and responding to their dreams—these things were also crucial to integrating dream wisdom into my life.

As time went on, I convened and attended dream circles, where listeners would offer different understandings of a single dream.

Over time, I began to see how sharing dreams connected people—and how attention to dreams added power, healing, and magic to people's lives and relationships. Some of my dreams, I discovered, held wisdom for others. And some of their dreams held wisdom for me. Some dreams seemed like they were meant for the whole community. I noticed patterns and images that seemed to repeat across dreams, across dreamers. I found myself feeling that, however different our dreams might be, everyone in my dreaming community was visiting the same place.

The kabbalists had the same intuition. The Zohar—a thirteenth-century Spanish treatise that envisions the unfolding aspects of God within creation—sees dreams as a journey we undertake at night. For the Zohar, the dreamscape is an actual Place, a whole world of sleeping souls: "When a person lies in bed, the soul goes out and wanders the world above, and enters the Place that she enters . . . When the person awakes, the soul tells the person about the dream."[1] The dream is a journey beyond the ordinary bounds of the self. On that journey, one can meet divine messengers, ancestors, demons. In this understanding of dreaming, the dreamworld is not an enclosed world inside the individual self, but a world of the soul—a world we all share.

Perhaps, when those ten different people dreamed about me all those years ago, the communal nature of dreams was exactly what I was supposed to understand. In Jewish tradition, the number ten indicates community and wholeness. (Ten is the minimum number of adults required to perform certain communal rituals, as well as the number of *sefirot* that make up the kabbalistic Tree of Life, representing the underlying structures, patterns, and processes of creation.) I have come to believe that dreamwork, to reach its full power, must be a communal practice. When we share our dreams as a community, we enrich our sense of interconnection and investment in each other's lives. Dreams are a human language that speaks from the depths and fringes of our being. And it is not only our own dreams that hold wisdom for us. All dreams are revelations of the mystery of existence. Every dream is a doorway to the deep.

This book is less a book about dreaming than it is a book of dreams, in which each dream is a portal to the dreamworld, allowing us to know ourselves, one another, and the world more deeply. Each dream is like a poem or a sacred text—it can be interpreted, but more importantly, its beauty can be felt, and its elemental power can heal and transform. Each dream retains the mystery of the dream landscape from which it came, and each one brings us back to the profound mystery of the cosmos in which we live. Delving into a dream, whether ours or someone else's, highlights not what we do or what we have, but who we are.

THE LANGUAGE OF DREAMS

Dreaming is woven into the fabric of our being. It is a core body function, shared with other mammals, experienced by humans for thousands of years. Before we had any semblance of human culture, we had dreams. Living by our dreams is a powerful and ancient practice, documented in tales and texts from thousands of years ago to the present day. To be guided by our dreams is to engage in a contemporary form of divination or prophecy, not from some far-away, disembodied deity, but from deep within the living earth. I believe that to be guided by our dreams is to be taught by the animate world, the Place/Presence that speaks to us in all of its subtle voices. We are ourselves composed of the elements of the world around us, deeply interwoven with the earth. That planetary voice speaks in us, and when we sleep, we may hear it even more clearly.

Current scientific research strongly suggests that dreams help us learn, innovate, and integrate new ideas. Our dreams show us what we can't fully perceive when we are awake and occupying our ordinary consciousness. If we take these uncanny perceptions seriously, we can be more permeable to the world and one another.

Regrettably, in our post-Freudian age, many have come to see dreams only as manifestations of personal psychology that reflect our hopes, fears, and repressed desires. One of my dear teachers and friends once told me: "Nothing is as boring as someone else's dream." This view suggests, perhaps, that while a dream may speak truth to the dreamer, it is irrelevant to anyone else. But to me, and in many ancient traditions, dreams aren't just personal messages: they're invitations to a timeless and ongoing collective journey. Dreams offer us an opportunity to visit the Place where truth unfolds through poignant and unpredictable images and voices, a Place our ancestors have visited before us.

I therefore understand dreams to communicate, not through symbolism—that is, by having some object or person stand in for a more abstract idea—but through a rhizomatic webwork of experience. That is, dreams are expressing not rarefied intellectual concepts, but interlinked, embodied relationships.

For example, consider the relationship of water with plant and animal life. Not only do plants and animals need water to survive, they are in fact mostly water. Or think of how water is connected to the actual experience of immersion. Water doesn't "symbolize" life, or immersion: rather, these phenomena are organically linked through our senses and experience of the world. A cave doesn't "symbolize" depth—the two are connected via our tangible experience and imagination. And particular people in our dreams aren't just "symbols" either: they and the feelings they evoke are part of our life-world.

Dreaming, in my view, is thus not about symbology. It's about exploring an intricate web of relationships and experiences, one that is more deeply embedded in us than our conscious abstract thoughts. This is an ecological view of dreaming: one in which our dreams connect us to the larger world of which we are a part. One might also call this a spiritual view of dreams—a view in which dreams help us to connect to a reality larger than ourselves. We might, in the language of Indigenous shamans, call that larger context the spirit world, or we might call it, in kabbalistic language, Shekhinah—Divine Presence. We might call it Mother Earth, or the Cosmos. We might even call it All That Is. Through our explorations of dreams, we will perhaps get glimmers of how we as finite beings connect, each in our own way, to this larger Being—and how that changes us.

UNDERTORAH:
THE RADICAL NATURE OF
DREAM PRACTICE

Coming from the Jewish tradition, I have used dream practice, in my life and in this book, to reclaim and renew early Israelite ways of meeting God. In the Bible, dream practice is a source of revelation. Before tablets were carved or scrolls were inscribed, Abraham dreamed of a flaming torch; Jacob dreamed of a ladder linking heaven and earth; Joseph dreamed of sheaves of wheat; Pharaoh dreamed of seven lean cows. These dreams are some of the first revelations within the Torah itself, in which the Divine "speaks" directly to an individual through their dreams.

But as the Bible goes on, the role of dreams begins to shift. In Numbers 12, God chastises the prophetess Miriam and her brother Aaron for questioning their brother Moses's leadership. God tells the pair that all prophets but Moses receive visions and dreams. But with Moses, God speaks clearly, "not in riddles." God then banishes Miriam (not Aaron—Miriam seems to be the main target for God's rage) from the camp for her critical words. This episode is clearly a rejection, or at best a marginalization, of dreaming prophets. This text marks a change, sometime in the biblical period, from the prophecy of dreams to the prophecy of Moses, which according to the text has greater clarity. Indeed, as Rodger Kamenetz notes in his book *The History of Last Night's Dream*, as soon as Torah became a fixed text, authorities (both in the Bible and in the Talmudic era) began to be nervous about treating dreams as revelation, lest they contradict the text.[2]

This shift in the preferred medium of prophetic transmission as recorded in the Bible is consistent with a larger historical development occurring throughout the Near East and the Levant. In *The Alphabet Versus the Goddess,* Leonard Shlain explores how the shift to alphabetic writing moved cultures toward text and away from images as a primary source of wisdom. This shift, Shlain believes, coincided with a devaluing of the feminine, and specifically a devaluing of the image of the Goddess.[3] This shift away from image is the same shift that moves the biblical authors toward textual prophecy and away from dreams. This is because, as theologian Natalie Weaver writes: "When *revelation* and *truth* are buttoned up in ancient texts and managed by sentinels of 'tradition,' dreaming is far too perilous, too personal, and too idiosyncratic to be received and directed as an important place of existential beingness."[4] The Zohar itself hints at something like this, saying: "Prophecy in the world is male, but the dream in the world is female."[5] Returning to the dream means returning to image, to the indeterminate, to the nonlinear, and to voices that have been suppressed or marginalized. If canonical revelation in Jewish tradition, which comes from above to below, is called Torah, we might call the dreamworld the Undertorah—a deep well of truth that lies hidden and bubbles up from beneath, shifting our notions of divinity and prophecy.

Not only are dreams not codified text, they are not even text. They are images, accompanied by feelings and voices. We may construct narratives out of them, but these narratives generally do not make "sense" according to our waking minds. Dream images, unmoored from linear thought and normative expectation, have the potential to introduce something original into our minds: a seed that can grow an idea, a transformation, even a new way of being. This is the essence of revelation.

Dreams do not speak from stone tablets in a voice of authority. They whisper in fragmented images, like a mosaic. They show us facets, faces, shards of the real. And when we "read" dreams, we do not all see the same thing. In the Talmud, Rabbi Bena'ah said that "there were twenty-four dream interpreters in Jerusalem. Once I dreamed a dream and went to all of them; each one offered a different interpretation, and they all came true."[6] In other words: a dream holds as many truths as we can find in it. Yet a dream also does not mean anything we read into it. Indeed, we might miss the crucial meaning of a dream if we avoid the emotions and images it presents. A dream has something real at its core: a seed of truth, even if that truth has many shoots that grow from it.

The Torah of dreams is thus less a Torah of words and concepts than it is a Torah of feeling, shape, and color. It is an embodied Torah, and it commands us not because of any imposed authority, but because of the intimacy of its message.

Returning to dreams as revelation through communal dream-work, a form of collective "oral Torah," means embracing a revelation that comes through a network of individuals rather than a single prophet or hierarchy—a web of intersecting visions that can give us insight into our lives, a way to know one another, a portal for entering the deep. When we treat dreams with care and respect, when we value one another's dreams and our own, when we record and read dreams as a reservoir of truth, we make it possible to access this field of revelation, the Undertorah—a unique realm that weaves consciousness with what lies beyond it. In this book I want to expose this field, and the diverse ways it manifests, in hopes that this portal will open for readers as well.

A dream is a gift. When we read or hear one, we're touching the sacred. So when you encounter dreams in this book, or when you encounter your own, I invite you to pause and take a breath. Enter the dream the way you would enter a sacred grove, a temple or cathedral. This dream has come up from the deep, from the under-girding of consciousness, from the place where everything touches everything else. Take a moment to appreciate the uniqueness of its beauty, or the starkness of its terror. The more you appreciate dreams in this way, the more you will find yourself living in the dreamworld even while awake—finding enchanted moments where beings interweave in strange ways, hearts reveal the delicate depths within, and journeys uncover mysterious treasures.

This book explores the idea that our dreams are a reflection of our intimate relationship with our bodies, each other, the sacred, and ultimately the cosmos. Every dream is a portal to that bedrock reality, those shifting images like tectonic plates below us. As we open portal after portal, we discover temples, guides, adversaries, healers. As poet Muriel Rukeyser says: "What shall we find? Energies, rhythms, journey. // Ways to discover. The song of the way in."[7]

Grounding in Our Dreams

It was the same dream every night just as I went to sleep . . . It was like drums beating so loud that you think they are your heartbeat. It was the Presence, whatever that means . . . The Presence was all around.

 —Patricia Bulkley[1]

The earth speaks to all of us, and if we listen we can understand.

 —Hayao Miyazaki[2]

Spring 1997, Jerusalem. In a dream, I find myself moving through a temple crowded with people. On the ground floor of the temple, there are ancient marble carvings. When I ascend to the top floor, I find, to my surprise, a weapons stockade. In the outer courtyard, there is a pile of stuffed animals for sale.

Then I venture into the stone tunnels under the temple. I come to caves with rock formations, and then to an underground river. The river bubbles as hot water spurts up through vents in the rocks.

Now I am with other companions, journeying together, but still I am afraid of becoming lost in the winding passages. My companions and I make our way down the river, deep into the earth, until we find a wide place like a delta, where the river branches in many directions.

Then the scene changes. I am looking at a beautifully drawn map of the caves and the underground river, a map that shows all the river's branches. The branches of the river look to me like lava vents around a volcano.

This dream, which I dreamed when I was studying in rabbinical school, provides a map of the dreamworld. The temple represents the human-made world. We find here expressions of human civilization: art and history (the carvings), violence and war (the weapons) and the emotional and sentimental realms (the stuffed animals). When we go beneath these objects, we find the elements that our creations are made from. We find stone and water. An underground river winds into the darkness and branches in many directions. This temple of the elements is much older and vaster than the temple up above. At this level of reality, in this place of wonder and terror, I connect to the power of the subconscious mind.

Then I am looking at a map—a record of the terrain I have just walked. This map shows the journey through the caves to the underground river, indicating that I am learning to navigate these layers of consciousness and chart them out for others. The map also shows me something I haven't yet seen: that the river is like lava vents stemming from a great volcano. The dreamworld, even in its vastness, has a single energy at its core: an elemental Presence that enlivens the dreamworld from below. We might say this Presence is the life-world in which the dreamer's consciousness is embedded. The fire of the volcano, the stone and air-filled tunnels of the caves, the water of the river—these are all signs of this Presence, which is Being itself.

The fact that the cave, the river, the heat all lie beneath the temple teaches me something important: that the sacred extends beyond the realms of human life. It precedes and surpasses us. The Great Temple is not a human-made building, but the cosmos itself, branching off into diverse realities, forging and reforging the elements that make life possible. In that elemental temple, that Place with a capital P, dwells the Presence that infuses the universe with life and meaning. Our dreams speak to us from that temple. We often dream in its elemental language, the language of the unconscious mind and the cosmic forces it senses within its depths.

New York City, 2011. I am sharing an apartment with my mother and a photographer I know. The two of them are lying in their beds. In a corner of the bedroom, I am writing notes, preparing a theology lecture for a class I am to give the next day. The title of the lecture is "Magmatheism." I intend the lecture to repair a belief system that is broken.

By the time I receive this dream, I am a rabbi and a mother. I have cofounded, with Taya Mâ Shere, the Kohenet Hebrew Priestess Institute, an organization that trains ritual and spiritual leaders in earth-based, embodied, feminist Jewish leadership. At the Kohenet Institute, we regard dreams as messengers of the sacred. I know when I wake up that an important dream has come to me, and that it is a sequel to the underground temple dream.

If magmatheism were a word, which it isn't, its meaning would be something like "belief in the divinity of molten rock." It sounds like a religion, or a type of faith. The dream tells me that magmatheism is meant as a healing for a broken way of thinking. Perhaps it is a repair for centuries of disembodied theology, a turning back toward the bedrock of embodied existence. The dream includes a mother (one who nurtures) and a photographer (one who sees), both in beds. One might say the dream invites the nurturing of dream images, a rekindling of relationship with the realms of sleep that connect us and direct us toward our origins.

When I wake up, I go immediately to Facebook and ask my friends to define magmatheism.

One says: "Magmatheism is the belief that divinity dwells below the ground and every once in a while erupts out gloriously."

Another says: "By studying the ways in which rock is liquid, we can understand the oneness of all things . . . Our separation is an illusion. We are part of the whole."

A third says: "Honoring the magnetic pull to earth."

A fourth says: "The unmanifest that creates the foundation of all life."

All of these visions of my dream are true. They remind me that the images we encounter in our dreams are from a wild, unfettered landscape—a kind of "underground," a deeper-than-ordinary

Chapter 1: Grounding in Our Dreams

reality where we can perceive directly what we only know dimly in our waking lives.

The message of "magmatheism" is that the wider cosmos is alive, and it is part of our extended selves. Our separation from nature is an illusion, and in dreams, where the ego's structuring consciousness is not so strong, we are able to transcend this illusion. We can see how our external worlds are ready and waiting to guide us along our paths, ultimately leading us back to the Source. Nature is ever guiding us home.

All of our encounters are meaningful. But the encounters we have in dreams are differently meaningful: wilder, unbridled. All realms of fantasy and imagery are possible in them. What appears in a dream doesn't have to appeal to reason. Dream imagery guides us, through the many streams available to it, to our purposes and paths. It hints to us of a conscious universe that connects and enlivens us, a fire under the mountain, a molten core. My encounter with this core offered me healing and transformation, a repair to my own belief system, and a renewed interest in and understanding of the power of dreams to guide us along the journey to our Source.

THE DOOR THAT DREAMS OPEN

What is a dream? A dream consists of images, emotions, and sensations that occur in the mind during sleep, often in the form of a story. Most dreams occur during what is known as REM (or "rapid eye movement"), a period of sleep characterized by flickering eye motion, faster pulse, and dreaming. People generally dream three to six times per night, but many dreams are forgotten. It is said that dreams are more likely to be remembered if an individual awakens during the REM stage. Many have found that their dreams are easier to remember when they establish a practice of recording them upon waking. Recording dreams on a regular basis stimulates our ability to remember them more often and more clearly. But this requires intention and discipline.

What are dreams for? Science suggests that dreams help us regain emotional health and peace.[3] Other studies suggest dreams help us creatively solve problems we couldn't solve while awake.[4] Still others suggest that dreams allow us to generalize our learning and think more flexibly.[5]

These things may be true. But why would running our recent memories and feelings through a kaleidoscopic image-generator give us inner peace or solve our problems? And why do dream images, no matter how strange and unlikely, often turn out to be so apt and prescient? Dreams sometimes speak from an intelligence that seems wiser than our waking selves.

Science supports the observation that dreams have a visionary quality. Science journalist Alice Robb notes that "when we dream, the logic centres of our brain—the frontal lobes—go dark, and chemicals associated with self-control, like serotonin and norepinephrine, drop. At the same time, the emotion centres light up; we have a perfect chemical canvas for dramatic, psychologically intense visions."[6]

We can think of this deepened visionary faculty as something we drop into naturally when we dream—the same way that we drop into a deeper state when we engage in spiritual practices like prayer, chant, or meditation. We might call this deepened vision a gift—a way to stay in touch with our Source.

I think of dreams not only as internal perceptions generated by my consciousness, but also as teaching and healing from Spirit sent to us during sleep. Dreams are part of the human spiritual faculty—that is, the innate human ability to perceive ourselves as part of something larger. The fluid imagination of the dreamworld allows us this wider perception.

Indigenous people have long known that dreams communicate wisdom and have preserved that living knowledge when other cultures have forgotten it. Many Native Americans work with dream presences as manifestations of spirit; some refer to powerful presences in dreams as *manitous* (guardian spirits or tutelary spirits).[7] Haudenosaunee (Iroquois) people understand dreams as "messages of the god within."[8] Indigenous Mexicans report sharing dreams around the breakfast table, while the Guajiro people of Colombia begin their day with the question: "How were your dreams?"[9]

In my own Jewish tradition, mystical texts tell that a dreamer's soul journeys to heavenly realms, contacts angels and demons, and receives counsel or admonishment. As we've noted, the Zohar, a thirteenth-century kabbalistic work, relates that "when a person is asleep in bed, the soul leaves and roams above . . . "[10] In other words, the dream is a journey of the soul, in which the soul encounters beings, places, and images that offer truth.

In my experience, a dream can offer advice—but rarely in a direct way, the way a friend or therapist does (though that sometimes happens). Mostly, dreams express themselves through images, bending characters and narratives into strange shapes we wouldn't see in waking life. The dream's images don't quite make sense, and yet they do. We might say that a dream communicates like e. e. cummings's poem "maggie and milly and molly and may":

> . . . milly befriended a stranded star
> whose rays five languid fingers were;
>
> and molly was chased by a horrible thing
> which raced sideways while blowing bubbles:and
>
> may came home with a smooth round stone
> as small as a world and as large as alone.
>
> For whatever we lose(like a you or a me)
> it's always ourselves we find in the sea[11]

A dream is like the sea in the poem: a place where we find ourselves. It has elements that are decipherable and others that don't make literal sense (like "as small as a world and as large as alone") but nevertheless each phrase offers a felt sense, a current of meaning. The oddities and enchantments of dreams create a current that one can follow and open up to. When we follow these currents, as I followed the underground river in my dream, we learn how to live in touch with ourselves and a greater living universe. In the words of the poem, "it's always ourselves we find in the sea."

We might say that dreams are the poems we and the Divine send one another.

THE GARDEN IN OUR DREAMS

In order to understand what a dream is trying to tell us, it is important to pay attention to the setting (something we will explore in much greater depth further on). While dreams are often very personal, many dreams have common elements, and certain settings tend to appear and reappear in the dreams of numerous people throughout history. For example, generations of people have recorded dreams that are set in a lush garden.

In sixteenth-century Tzfat, in the Galilee, a Jewish woman named Merchavah dreamed of walking in a garden. Rabbi Hayyim Vital, her teacher, recorded her dream, in which he also appeared. He wrote: "The trees there smelled of myrrh and aloe wood . . . Pools of water flowed in the garden and ornamental fountains emerged from them, flowing with water . . . She looked up and saw a noble woman, lovely and voluptuous, sitting in a high attic . . . The dreamer saw me standing next to her, and I was saying to her: 'Here, this is the true place.'"[12]

This gorgeous dream is connected to the beliefs of the kabbalists. For Merchavah and for Hayyim Vital, it would have been clear that the garden in the dream was the divine world, and that the woman in the high attic was Shekhinah, Divine Presence. Hayyim Vital also records his own dreams of that woman and her garden. In his dream, a woman "as beautiful as the sun" helped him climb a ladder, step through a fiery portal, and enter "a wondrous yard with flowing rivers and fragrant, lush, verdant groves of fruit trees and tall shade trees."[13]

This image of the woman and garden who together embody Divine Presence is central to the Jewish mystical imagination. For the kabbalists, God has multiple aspects with different energies. One of the most important forms of God is the Presence, or the tangible divine energy within all physical substance. In Hebrew, this Presence is called Shekhinah (literally, Indwelling). Kabbalists understand this Presence as a feminine facet of God that receives the energy of all of the hidden realms and manifests that energy as the abundance of forms in the physical world. "The Shekhinah is in charge of all the blessings of the world, and from Her flow blessings for all."[14]

What the kabbalists are expressing, in contemporary terms, is an ecological view in which the world is a divine manifestation—a conscious, loving container within which life can unfold. Some contemporary Jewish mystics, like Rabbi Zalman Schachter-Shalomi and Rabbi Leah Novick, have compared this way of thinking to Gaia consciousness—the notion of a sentient world that has a consciousness of itself as a whole being.[15]

What I find most powerful and compelling about the Presence of the kabbalists is that She (or He, or They, since gender doesn't fully apply here) is not only an Entity but also a Place: the ground of being within which we live and move. Kabbalists speak of this Presence/Place as the Beloved, or the Bride, of the transcendent God. She is mother, garden, orchard, sea, temple, earth itself. She is the body of creation, the web of life, and "all things are united in Her."[16] I imagine the mystics who encounter the Shekhinah are experiencing something very much like what I experience when I leave my house and walk in Central Park. I see that the trees, water, stones and light are all uniquely themselves, and yet they are all part of a greater unity: a life-world that surrounds and informs me at every moment. This world is alive and seeks to be in dialogue with me. And this is how I read dreams: as a seeking-toward-dialogue from a Presence embodied in the whole of being—and perhaps also our seeking back.

Dream images show us our fundamental connection to Being—to the world of plants, animals, earth and stars, what David Abram calls the "more-than-human world."[17] We can never fully perceive the Being that holds us: we can't see the electrons or touch the stars that send their light to us from such a great distance. Nor can we see the cosmos inside us, the inner workings of our neurons, blood, muscle, and bone. These things are what author and ecologist Stephan Harding calls "the scientific 'invisibles'—the atoms, microbes and feedback relationships that make up the astonishing body of our living Earth."[18] Yet somewhere within us we viscerally know the truth of our origins: that we are an organic particle of a vast living cosmos we can barely comprehend. As mystic and dreamworker Catherine Shainberg has written, "Dreaming is the language of the body."[19] And our bodies are interwoven with the world's larger body.

Usually we think we are separate from that "natural world," but when we dream, it is as if someone has opened a back door through which we can circumvent our ordinary isolated consciousness and touch the life force of which we are a part. And when we do touch that great power, it touches back: we often feel a sense of love and desire, coming from what David Abram calls an "enigmatic cosmos" that speaks to us in "a myriad of tongues."[20] The Zohar teaches that "at the time of sleeping ... every person's soul goes out and rises up, and the souls conceal themselves inside Shekhinah."[21] The Place of the dream, its landscape as well as its creatures, is a communication from the All.

In the contemporary West, we often think of dreams as the language of one's own personal psychology, the "psyche" or the "soul." Every character in a dream, we are told, is a reflection of us. For example, Michael Lennox writes: "Dream work . . . is entirely about self-investigation."[22] If we subscribe to Jungian theories, we might also see dreams as reflections of a collective human psychology: the realm of archetypes.[23] All of these dream levels have power. But what if dreams are not so self-centered? As dreamworker Stephen Aizenstat writes, "Dream figures and images do not necessarily originate within the personal psyche of the dreamer."[24] Dreams also open up our connection to what is larger than us. Aizenstat calls the cosmic aspect of dreams the "ecological consciousness" or the "world unconscious."[25] We might call this the elemental aspect of the dream, where we encounter the great and mysterious powers within and all around us.

THE SEARCH FOR DREAM HEALING

A dream is a powerful experience in and of itself. It doesn't need to be analyzed, categorized, or understood to make an impact. We don't need our dreams interpreted as much as we need them witnessed. And yet it's beneficial to consider what gifts a dream has brought us, because dreams have the power to change our lives in the waking world. As dreamworker Rodger Kamenetz and many others have noted, the images in dreams are a kind of medicine.[26] Because dreams help us perceive ourselves as part of something larger, they are a balm for the things that ail our egoic selves: fear, resentment, inhibition, apathy, regret. And because they are a "back door" out of our ordinary consciousness, they can grant us a fuller vision of ourselves. They come to us when we are asleep, in a state of surrender, open to suggestion, and they offer us new ways of being that we can then try to integrate into our lives. Dreams, with their visionary quality, bring to light what is wounded, broken, or forgotten in us and our world, and show us paths to repair, remembrance, and healing.

Let me explain by sharing a dream from a woman I'll call Sasha, who is a healer and a kohenet ordained by the Kohenet Hebrew Priestess Institute.[27] Sasha shared this dream with me because I was the teacher in her dream. There is a talmudic tradition that dreams others dream about you have a message for you.[28] This dream of Sasha's taught me a great deal about dream healing.

My teacher has called me to meet her at a cathedral in the middle of the night because, she says, "it has the best access to the fields." She tells me that there are tangles or disruptions in the fields we work with. She raises her hands and pulls down a series of large screens, like the maps or projection screens from school; they are maps of the nine layers of being/time/space. She says the ninth layer, which is the top, is the easiest to read because it is just constellations—lines and dots—but you can see from this layer that there is a major disruption.

I say that I often work in the second and third layers, which are the pipes and ductwork. We both agree that when something seems off, the issue is usually located there, in the second and third layer. She says: "Go."

I dive underground, through dirt and rootlets to a layer of time and space with very low ceilings and a dirt and stone floor. I know I am in the foundations of somewhere very sacred. There are hordes of people wandering around, muttering and lost. I take a breath and then begin to push them away with my hands, saying: "Out!

Out! Out! Return! Return!" Then I find what
looks like a finger sticking out of the ground,
and a hump of someone's back, just barely vis-
ible under the earth. I talk to my teacher in
my mind, saying that there is a being stuck
between the worlds. He is in Shtiyah, *I say.*

This being has stuck his finger in a hole and
it is affecting the flow of the energies. Nothing
can come in or out of the hole. I know I need to
dislodge this massive creature, but first I need
to understand him. This being is not exactly
malevolent, but certainly disregulated and dis-
regulating. I need to pull him out but I know he
is much too heavy for me. The being is water-
logged and dense with the eating of earth. My
heart is racing. It feels urgent, but I don't know
what to do. I wake up in a sweat. I write down
the word Shtiyah.

In this dream, the teacher invites Sasha to a cathedral where there is good access to the "fields"—the energetic maps of reality. In Jewish mystical tradition, one of the names for Shekhinah is the Field, and the interpenetrating realms of space, time, and sentience are explicitly described in an ancient Jewish book known as the Book of Creation, or Sefer Yetzirah.[29] Just as Jacob dreamed of a ladder connecting all elements of reality, Sasha dreams of a series of cosmic fields, each one only reachable from the other, like steps. She dreams her own version of the Place.

The teacher begins with the highest field: the ninth field, where Reality appears as simple dots and dashes. On this level, the teacher indicates a disturbance that must be repaired. Sasha then identifies herself as someone who works on levels "two and three," levels where hands-on work can be done, where there are "pipes and ducts"—energy channels that might be clogged. The dreamer then dives underground and finds herself in a "sacred foundation" beneath the earth, another vision of the underground temple. First, she sees lost people wandering around and attempts to expel them. Then, she finds a being stuck between the worlds. She identifies this between-place as *Shtiyah*.

The term *Shtiyah* is a real term, though Sasha didn't know this until she looked the term up later. In Jewish legend, the *Even Shtiyah*, or Stone of Foundation, is the stone from which God began to create the world. It is the place where all things arise from one thing. A legend relates:

> Just as the fetus in its mother's womb starts at the navel and spreads out this way and that way to the four directions, so too the Holy One made the world, making the Stone of Foundation first and from it spreading out the world. It is called the Stone of Foundation for from it the Holy One began to create the world.[30]

According to the Talmud, this stone sits beneath the Holy of Holies. It is the foundation of the Temple, the elemental root of all. On that spot, the stone holds back the primordial waters. It is a portal to the deep. This stone appeared in Sasha's dream as an embodiment of the human predicament of living between worlds: the mundane realm and the realm of the cosmic whole.

In Sasha's dream, someone has gotten into this passageway and blocked it. His finger is stuck in the hole, like the finger of the Dutch boy in the dike. Sasha doesn't know what to do to remove the blockage, but she knows that the entity cannot remain in the passage between the worlds. She understands it is her task to clear the way so healing flow can happen. This is true in her waking life: she is a healer, of herself and others, and the dream has given her a picture of her work in the world. She is to remove blockages, help lost pieces of the self return home, and coax our stuck selves out of their hiding places.

In the dream, there are multiple levels of reality. On Level Nine, there are archetypal patterns. This is the layer of "constellations"—of webs of related phenomena. On Levels Two and Three, there is "plumbing"—the messy details. This is more or less true of our dreams, and our lives as well. Dreams can show us both Level Nine—the larger patterns we are part of—and Levels Two and Three—the particular problems and blockages that face us. Dream healing can happen on a "broad" level via images that express the essence of our souls and the cosmos of which they are a part, and on a "close-up" level via images that show us what is broken, or what is in need of healing in our lives.

Sasha learns that in order to dislodge the being stuck between the worlds, she first needs to understand it. This is also dream wisdom. When we try to understand the story dreams tell us, we may be able to enact the healing they offer. We can try to understand the dream by asking ourselves what it is that we perceive, or by asking others for help. If we lived in a society that took dreams seriously, we would be looking to dreams to show us solutions for the small and large problems we live with but don't know how to address.

Meredith Sabini, a Jungian psychologist who works with dreams and the earth, writes: "Were we living in a viable traditional culture during a time of upheaval such as our own, we would be gathering regularly to hear and discuss dreams . . . Dreaming itself *is* a natural resource, abundant and self-renewing."[31] Yet even though many of us have lost the art of sacred dreaming, we can return to our ancestors' dreaming practices and receive wisdom in our own time. Dreams can and must be an ally to us as we struggle with a changing and challenged world.

We have help in doing this work: dream guides, healers, and teachers who invite us, provoke us, and let us be vulnerable. We have help from dream places—the "temples" in the dream, which evoke our awe and curiosity. Even when a dream is scary or troubling, there may be places in the dream that connect us to the healing Place and its abundant Presence. Even when the culture around us disconnects us from the earth and each other, the dreams show us another way. We are all connected at our root to the power and sanctity of the animate cosmos. The underground temple is never far away. We can remember and return.

CHAPTER 2

Dreaming
the Journey

A person can be asleep in one place yet dream
of far-away places.

—Talmud[1]

In the sixteenth century, in the city of Tzfat, the kabbalistic sage Hayyim Vital recorded his son Shmuel's dream, a strange journey upon which Shmuel was accompanied by angels and demons:

> We descended into the pit which was in the courtyard and at the bottom of the pit was a hole. We exited from there and we entered a lovely house with fine couches and many windows. Each window opened to a different direction and they exited to the place one wished to go. We went out one window and we went to the Mediterranean Sea and in one corner of the sea there was a great darkness. In the midst of the darkness was a small hole, the size of a pomegranate, and in it was a light, like a burning candle.

Through this complex pathway, an angel tells him, angels ascend to bring messages to humans.[2]

In so many dreams, we keep trying to get somewhere. Sometimes we're trying to catch a plane and have too much baggage, or don't have our ticket. Sometimes we keep changing trains, or searching through a house for a person or a room. Where are we trying to go? What is our frenetic traveling supposed to accomplish?

Certainly all this activity reflects our hyperbusy days as humans in the twenty-first century. Yet we can also choose to understand these dreams as journey dreams, in which we are searching for something bigger and more meaningful than our mundane days have to offer.[3] We might say that we are searching for the entrance to the Place: the ground of being, the sacred cosmos of which we are always subconsciously aware. Our dreams allow us to relax the sense of our separate consciousness and enter a more visionary state, where we can discover our innate connection to Being.

Shmuel's dream, more than most, shows us the nature of this journey. He descends to a pit, then to a beautiful home, then to the sea, then to the small hole with a light inside. He is told this pathway is the road of the angels—and it is. The path we search for in dreams guides us to messages from the beyond. But it's not always easy to find. When I have a dream in which I am on a train or a plane or in a complex warren of alleyways, I know this dream reflects my waking anxieties. Yet I also understand such a dream to be a subconscious search for meaning, for connection, for comfort—for the underground temple where I can meet the cosmos that lies beyond my limited consciousness.

THE SPACE BEYOND: JOURNEY DREAMS
THAT TAKE US PLACES

Our journey dreams often take place in the everyday world of our houses, workplaces, or familiar buildings. After all, humans in the US (for example) spend 90 percent of our time inside, on average.[4] But then, as we progress on our dream journey, we may begin to encounter spaces that do not feel entirely ordinary.

When I was a child, I had a recurring dream in which I would go into my closet. High up in the closet was a little door, and when I climbed up and passed through the door, there would be a huge, light-filled building like a shopping mall, with many niches and alcoves. I loved this dream; it gave me a sense of magic and adventure. Like Shmuel's dream, the journey took me from an ordinary space (my bedroom) into an extraordinary space (the light-filled mall). When I began to ask others about the architecture of their dreams, I discovered that dreams in which an ordinary space holds hidden secrets are not unusual. Such dreams suggest an initiation into the awareness that our world is bigger and more magical than our waking minds imagine.

Joseph, a computer programmer, musician, and mystic, shared with me a dream in which he was walking through an ordinary, modern campus where people learned magic.

> *Then I look up. Something like a classical uni-*
> *versity, with multiple wings, cloisters, court-*
> *yards, and breezeways is hanging in the sky.*
> *The "campus" I saw before was simply the*
> *place where this vast edifice intersects with the*
> *ground. Although blue sky is visible through it,*
> *it appears to just keep going indefinitely. I enter*
> *the building and begin climbing stairs, passing*
> *through hallways, lounges, and classrooms. I*
> *am looking for something—a way into the upper*
> *world, a place of refuge, a shrine.*

Joseph's dream proceeds in a similar way to Shmuel's dream hundreds of years before. A relatively mundane space turns into a supernatural space. As Joseph climbs stairs through the campus in the sky, he is approaching the Place: that is, he is approaching his own awareness of the complex and vibrant cosmos, so much wilder and more extraordinary than our minds can normally hold. He is becoming aware of the magic of the cosmos.

Of course, our journey dreams don't always get us to floating castles. Often they run us in circles. But the journey dream is *trying* to get us somewhere. It is trying to get us to the sacred innermost Place where we can connect to the Presence. We may be looking for our Source, for renewal, for inspiration, or for healing. The paths we travel in our dreams are the same paths that, in the language of Shmuel's dream, angels take to bear us messages.

A ROOM OF ONE'S OWN:
FINDING GIFTS ON THE JOURNEY

Sometimes we enter a dream and get stuck in the loop of the journey. For example, it's not uncommon for me to find myself in an airport where I wait and wait in line, but never get to the right gate—or on a dock where I run to make the ferry, but arrive just as it leaves. However, if we patiently watch these frustrating dreams over time, we will eventually arrive somewhere. And that some-where, whether mundane or marvelous, may tell us something important about our gifts, resources, fears, or vulnerabilities. This wisdom can help us, in waking and dreaming life, to get past the roadblocks in our journeys.

This journey dream comes from Iris, a kohenet living in the southwestern US. This dream is entirely contained in human spaces, and yet it suggests a movement toward something deeper.

> I am walking through a tunnel, a basement hall with no windows. I notice that I am skating in smooth, easy motions. I don't know how my shoes have become roller skates, but I love it. The motion of my body feels so good, and the movement is comfortable and powerful. I come to a few stairs, and people offer to help me, but I don't need help. Somehow it is easy to walk up the stairs on the skates.
>
> Then I am in a hospital. I go over to the recep-tion desk, where there is a very pleasant man. I explain I am no longer on the medical staff, but am being treated there. I don't remember my room number, and have some concerns that this staff member won't tell me what it is, since I have no ID with me. The man finds no prob-

lem with my request, and gives me my room
number willingly. It is always okay to ask, he
says.

In her dream, Iris is roller-skating, and it feels good. She loves the feeling of movement, competence, and power. When Iris and I work the dream, she agrees that the roller-skating moment embodies ease and joy for her. I invite her to reexperience the joy of roller-skating—to integrate into herself that moment of feeling alive.

For Iris, the underground temple is a hospital, and soon she meets a man on the hospital staff. Here comes the nervous part of the dream: Iris is trying to establish her identity and her credentials for being there. I relate; I, too, often lose my ID in a dream. I wonder if perhaps we fumble for our paperwork in dreams because we are trying to recover the identity of our deeper selves.

Iris tells the kind receptionist that she used to be on the staff and is now being treated there. Based on this, we might say that Iris is both a healer and in need of healing. It seems Iris has come to the right place, because even though she has no ID with her, the man helps her find her room, and reassures her that it is okay to ask. This welcoming man may be connected to the guardian/guide figures we will discuss in Chapter Four. He knows the way to where Iris needs to go: her own room, a place designated specifically for her.

Iris tells me she likes the man a lot. When I ask what she likes about him, she says it is good to know she can receive help, that there is a room available for her healing. Receiving the man's care and concern, and a space reserved especially for her, makes her feel not alone in the universe. I invite Iris to go back to that man in future meditations—to feel his care for her as he tells her she has a room, and it is okay to ask where it is. The dream guide offers Iris the insight that she has a place in the world, a room that is entirely her own.

THE INFINITE STAIRCASE:
DREAMS THAT DIVERT US IN
THE RIGHT DIRECTION

In journey dreams, we may be at peace or troubled, awed or confused, frustrated or pleased. There are moments when we know we are journeying toward something numinous and sacred, and there may be moments when we seem to be getting nowhere. Sometimes in a journey dream, losing our way is how we find ourselves.

The theme of losing one's way to find one's "place" is illustrated beautifully in this journey dream from a rabbi I'll call Gordon:

> *I am walking through a crowded, colorful, chaotic street with a small group. The group idolizes a leader who teaches a simple way to reach spiritual enlightenment. Together, we walk toward his high-rise apartment.*
>
> *I separate from the group, needing to find my own way—or maybe to find a quicker way, because I know that to arrive early means preferential treatment. Knowing full well that the group will take the elevator, I take the stairs. I can run faster than the elevator and it feels like a challenge to beat a mechanical device with my own strength and willpower.*
>
> *But the stairwell is confusing: it seems to lead nowhere, spiraling out in an infinite loop, like an Escher drawing. Disconnected stair fragments go up and down without a normal sequence.*
>
> *Within the stairwell I see an imbalanced washer-dryer teetering on the edge of the stairs. I*

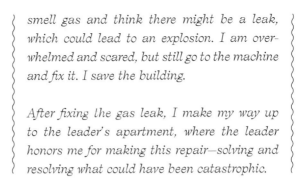

smell gas and think there might be a leak, which could lead to an explosion. I am overwhelmed and scared, but still go to the machine and fix it. I save the building.

After fixing the gas leak, I make my way up to the leader's apartment, where the leader honors me for making this repair—solving and resolving what could have been catastrophic.

In this dream Gordon is trying to prove himself to his spiritual teacher by getting to the chosen destination first. But the dream leads him in a different, unexpected direction. As with many journey dreams, the dream moves from ordinary space to extraordinary space: a stairwell that winds in an infinite loop. The staircase doesn't lead Gordon to his teacher's apartment, but to a task he needs to fulfill.

When Gordon discovers the washer-dryer with a gas leak in the spiraling stairwell, he could ignore it and keep searching for his teacher's apartment, his intended destination. But he doesn't. He takes time out of his journey to fix the broken machine, and thereby saves the building. In the end, the spiritual leader honors Gordon, not for getting to the apartment first, but for his concern for others' safety and for using his practical gifts to solve a dangerous problem.

Gordon, an environmentalist, worked with this dream in a circle that I led, and the group suggested to him that the dream invited him to trust himself as a "repairer." Gordon spoke to us of his pride in being able to fix things and solve problems, and of his commitment to healing the world. The journey dream showed him which of his gifts he can rely on as he journeys deeper into the dreamworld (and the waking world as well).

A dream journey may not always deliver us to our desired destination. Sometimes it cuts off awkwardly, and sometimes it seems like more of an "episode" than a whole movie. But even so, our experience on these journeys may give us clues about who we are, what our gifts are, and what our fears are. We have to be on the lookout, in our dreams, for these gifts. We also have to be mindful that sometimes "failing," in a dream, can mean arriving at a deeper victory. As we follow such dreams, we may develop new capacities for awareness so we can take further steps toward our larger quest.

SEEKING MEANING
IN A DREAM JOURNEY

So if we've had a journey dream, what is it for? What do we do with it? Looking into a journey dream, we can reflect on what the dream is telling us about our gifts and challenges, or consider the wisdom it is sharing about how to move forward. Working with a journey dream can also mean noticing where the dream points us deeper, into spaces of connection, awe, or beauty.

Let's use one dream as an example of how to seek meaning in a journey dream. Naomi, an educator and kohenet, shared with me a recurring dream from her childhood that took place "in three different phases." She had remembered the dream because of its power and clarity.

> *In the first phase I am enjoying a peaceful stroll through the woods near my childhood home. Sometimes I am alone. Sometimes I am with my mother. We're not focused on arriving anywhere; there's just an innate sense that this is what we are supposed to be doing right now.*
>
> *In the second phase, after walking for some time, I encounter a strange black wall that rises high up into the forest. On its surface are a*

variety of brightly-colored handles, chains, and other objects, which I use to start climbing the wall. It's a hard climb, and I have to take time to choose each handhold and foothold as I go up. Again, I'm thinking about what I'm doing in the moment rather than wondering where I am going.

In the third phase, when I finally reach the top, I arrive at my grandparents' house in Omaha, Nebraska. Their living room wall now opens up into the sky, and I climb in through the hole. My grandparents are overjoyed to see me and we proceed with the visit as if nothing strange had happened.

When I asked Naomi what the dream had come to tell her, she replied:

> I feel like the wisdom offered to me by the dream is that every single goal or achievment in life will require phases of effort . . . So much of life is spent in these in-between times where you are trying to get somewhere. Those parts are real life too and shouldn't be overlooked.

In other words, Naomi's dream was teaching her about the nature of the journey itself: that the journey *is* the destination. We cannot always be waiting for the perfect end to the story. The moments that occur along the way to our goals are equally important and should not be dismissed or overlooked.

Noting that journey dreams sometimes show us our gifts and challenges, I suggested to Naomi that the dream calls her attention to her gifts of persistence and fortitude. The child Naomi doesn't give up halfway up the wall, and neither does the adult Naomi give up on her dreams and desires. Family is a core value for Naomi as well, and this is reflected in her dream as her destination is a place where her family loves and welcomes her.

Naomi's dream also connects her to the earth—the peaceful forest—and the sky, to which she ascends using the climbing wall. The wall with its handholds represents her life challenges—"completing college and graduate school, becoming a mother, getting divorced and remarried again, moving our household from place to place." Yet the forest all around gives her a sense of peace and rightness: "This is what we are supposed to be doing right now." And of course, the grandparents' house is Naomi's version of the Place, a haven that radiates Presence, warmth, and love—giving her a sense of meaning and belonging to something greater than herself.

Many dreams are journey dreams, where we are traveling, and perhaps searching for Presence. It may be that you have an immediate "hit" about what a dream is telling you as soon as you wake up, or it might come to you later. Regardless, when you wake up from a journey dream, whether it seemed to have a final destination or not, it's good to record it so that you can remember it and work with it later. It's also good to have a trusted friend, counselor, or dream circle to share the dream with, because sometimes someone else will see something in the dream that you have missed. In either case, *the process of reflecting on a dream, whether alone in writing or in conversation with others, is a key to recovering its hidden blessing and wisdom.*

Begin by noticing the details. Where do you begin? Where are you trying to get to? Where do you end up? Whom do you meet along the way? What ordeals or opportunities do you encounter? What Place (or Presence), if any, is at the end of the journey? What does all this tell you about what matters? Look at the dream like a sacred text: everything in it means something. Allow yourself to free-associate and see what comes up for you around the images in the dream.

Notice the feelings that come up in the dream as well as the images and narratives. Are there images that feel especially powerful to you? Moments where deep emotion arises? What do these images or moments tell you? Dreamworker Mary Jo Heyen says that "dreams are feelings waiting to be felt."[5] What feelings want to be felt in your dream?

What parts of the dream suggest gifts you can celebrate, or challenges you might need to watch out for?

These gifts—like Gordon's problem-solving or Naomi's persistence and family connection—can help us to find meaning, strength, and vibrant life in our waking experience as well. And the challenges—like the strange black wall—can tell us something about what we are facing in our lives.

Are there any images, characters, feelings, or patterns that connect this dream to previous dreams? If so, look at the dreams side by side and see what else you can learn. Dream journeys tend to repeat, at least in their broad strokes. Some people often dream of misplacing their ticket, others of having baggage that's too heavy. If you're seeing a pattern, how might this pattern reflect what's happening in your waking world?

Journey dreams, like Naomi's dream, sometimes get us closer to where we want to be. You may want to reflect on how the dream might be bringing you closer to Presence. Is there a "grandparents' house" or other destination that feels like it brings you deeper?

Most importantly, don't be frustrated if your journey dreams don't have a destination. They are still doing the work, spiritually speaking, of getting you where you need to go. The dreamworld isn't linear, so don't expect linearity. Just go along for the ride.

Elemental Portals to the Presence

We are situated in the land in much the same way that characters are situated in a story . . . Along with the other animals, the stones, the trees, and the clouds, we ourselves are characters within a huge story that is visibly unfolding all around us, participants within the vast imagination, or Dreaming, of the world.

—David Abram[1]

Place is critical. It's not just the embodied imagination, it's the emplaced imagination. Places want to be in relationship with us and we're the ones who have held ourselves back.

—Sharon Blackie[2]

Sometimes, as we go along in our dream journeys, we come to a place that is so beautiful, powerful, or mysterious that it startles us. This place may be different for each one of us, and can be different from dream to dream. Often, such a place is marked by powerful elemental forces—as if the cosmos itself is attempting to enter our consciousness and speak to us in our dreams.

In 1 Kings 19, Elijah encounters such a place. As he stands on a mountain, he sees a great and mighty wind, an earthquake, and a fire, and then hears a still, small voice. While Elijah says that "God was not in the wind," in fact, the elements he encounters—wind, earth, and fire—*prepare and invite him* to come closer to Presence. They are portals for sacred experience. So too, in the ancient Temple, the washing basin, the *menorah* (lamp), and the incense that sends smoke into the air are elemental gateways to encountering Presence.

In our dreams, we too may encounter elements of the kind that Elijah encountered: fire, water, wind, or earth. When we do, it is a sign that the Presence is close by. These elemental dream encounters can provide healing and connection, as well as invite us into deeper awareness of the sentience of our waking-world surroundings. As scientist Stephan Harding writes, we need to rediscover and embody "a deep sense of participating in a cosmos suffused with intelligence, beauty, intrinsic value and profound meaning."[3] Elemental portals within our dreams may allow us to return to this sense of Presence/Place.

In fact, Robert Moss suggests that dream places—landscapes, schools, places of initiation—are real places, where we do real work toward our own healing and enlightenment. Within these places, we become "engineers of the imaginal realms."[4] Our dream consciousness generates the exact places we need to visit in order to grow, change, and heal. The elemental forces we encounter within such places are portals designed especially for us, to bring us deeper into Presence.

Within this chapter you'll find examples of these elemental portals. As you read these dreams, notice where you've found such portals in your own dreams, and consider what they looked, sounded, or felt like for you. Some of us are drawn to water, others to fire, still others to stones. The elements are diverse, but as the ancient Sefer Yetzirah (Book of Creation) teaches us, they all "emerge from a single Name."[5]

EARTH: THE TREE OF LIFE

The Tree of Life with its blossoming branches stands in the center and overshadows all of Eden. It has fifteen thousand fruits, and each one of them is unique. No taste, smell, or image of any one of its fruits is remotely like the other.

—Masechet Gan Eden[6]

The Tree of Life [was] the foundation for all that was above and below ... It was the universal representation of all that exists ... Everything was interconnected and all of the roots led back to one source.

—Brynn Myers[7]

The kabbalah tells how the Tree of Life unfolds from heaven and stretches down to earth—a web of divine aspects through which radiance flows from the One to all creatures. The Norse Yggdrasil, the world-tree, connects all the nine worlds; "no one knows from where its roots run."[8] The Mayans say there are four world-trees in each of the four directions. In Egypt, the gods emerge from a sacred tree. In India, the Eternal Banyan Tree survives all catastrophes, and in Persian myths, the Gaokerena world-tree unfolds both good and evil. In these myths and legends, the Tree is a depiction of the living universe as a single organism branching into myriad realities.

Sometimes in our dreams, the temple appears to us as a tree. People have told me dreams of walking through tunnels of trees and branches, of discovering doorways into trees, of coming upon trees whose branches hover, linked to the trunk by only a thread. The World-Tree we see in our dreams and our sacred stories is a species-wide intuition of the living and connected nature of reality. Trees, with their forks and branches stretching in different directions, help us explain to ourselves how such a diverse and branching world can be one being, one interdependent web of life. In my experience, tree dreams teach us about interconnection, about our relationship with the larger world. Here are two dreams that bring us into intimate contact with the World-Tree.

Irene, an academic who lives in Berlin, dreamed this dream of the Tree of Life:

> *My friend and I are walking through a forest. The earth is brown and soft below our feet. The tree branches are green and form a protective roof over our heads.*
>
> *To my left, I note an opening in a tree. I delve into it, and find a hollow as big as the lobby of a hotel. I am inside the biggest tree one can imagine—inside the tree's brain. Its giant consciousness is deep and green and brown: a dark, protective, yet somehow open and beautiful space. I have never seen or felt or been surrounded by something more beautiful than this. This openness of spirit/brain is somehow connected with my brain/me. It is me, I am it: this great giant connectedness.*

> *In the next second, I look out from within the*
> *hall inside the giant tree-trunk, and I see New*
> *York City below. The tree is as high as the Em-*
> *pire State Building. I realize that I must have*
> *taken an elevator to get that high. Amazed, I*
> *wake up, sorry the dream is over.*

Irene's journey into the forest becomes a foray into a massive tree. The tree is alive: a being with a porous mind that both accepts and protects. Irene can intimately sense the immense conscious-ness of the huge tree, and comes to understand that the tree is connected to her consciousness as well: "It is me, I am it." She instinctively recognizes the beauty of this being.

From inside the tree, Irene is able to look out and see New York City below. The tree is higher than the buildings: Irene feels and knows that the tree is so much bigger than what humans have made. The World-Tree has revealed itself to her in the dream. She has found her portal to the Presence.

THE TREE OF LIFE
AND THE COSMOS WITHIN

Sometimes our encounters with the Tree of Life help us realize that we, too, are an integral part of the cosmos. Clare, a rabbi of New York City, tells of an "epic dream" of hers from fifteen years ago. In the dream, she wakes up suspended on a square of canvas hung in a canopy of graceful trees. Easing herself onto a branch, she unties the canvas, holds onto two of its ends, and jumps.

> *The wind catches me instantly, and I go up*
> *in the air rather than down. I sail through the*
> *trees, pulling with one hand or the other to steer*
> *around the trunks, and rise and fall with the*
> *wind. For several minutes all I am aware of*

is the elation of flying and the endlessness of the forest. I begin to sing, joyfully, and realize quickly that I am not alone; another voice is harmonizing with me. Then there is another voice, and then several.

As she flies through the air, Clare joins in the many-voiced song of the trees, and discovers that even after she sails over the forest and comes to hills and plains, the song continues. "I felt like I was making the words up as I was going along, or perhaps that someone else was making them up and somehow I knew exactly what to sing." As the wind dies down and night falls, Clare lands on a hill and watches the sunset. It's cold, and she searches for a place to get warm.

On the side of the hill is a small window, through which I can see a potbellied stove and a kettle in a small room. When I reach the bottom of the hill, I realize that the roots of a tree have grown down the sides of the hill, creating a dome which had been completely hollowed out. I find a hidden, mossy door, and I walk inside.

The single, round room is warm and smells like earth. Everything is brown, different shades that shift as I look at them. There is no furniture, but around the entire room is a deep ledge carved into the earth at waist height, and part of the ledge is piled up with quilts and blankets. Another section of the ledge holds several brown mugs and plates, stacked neatly on the dirt. The stove in the middle of the room has a small fire, the only source of light, but the whole room glows bronze and copper and beautiful.

Chapter 3: Elemental Portals to the Presence

The door is a portal to a room within the tree itself, where the "furniture" is made of earth. The dreamer has come to the "roots" of things. "Roots" implies foundations and connection to the earth, and the rest of the dream bears out these themes.

> *The kettle begins to whistle. I peek inside. It smells like Earl Grey tea and hot cocoa, and I carry the kettle carefully to the ledge and pour a mugful. Just as I am about to put the kettle down, a voice behind me says, "Pour a cup for me as well." I pour the second cup without looking to see who has asked, then turn around.*
>
> *Standing just inside the door is a person wrapped in many layers of blankets and scarves. Their skin is the color of dark chocolate, and they have the most beautiful face I've ever seen. Silently, I hand over the hot cocoa and smile. One moment he looks like a woman, the next moment I am sure she is a man. But after taking a deep drink of her hot cocoa, he smiles at me and says: "Both, or neither, if you prefer."*
>
> *"What is your name?" I finally manage to ask, and she replies "Sayyid." He finishes the hot chocolate and hands the cup back to me, and then begins to take off many layers of clothing. As she takes off each scarf, he holds it up toward the ceiling, and it is absorbed by the tree. Her gloves melt into a wall. Then he hands his overcoat to the door, and it becomes part of the door. Finally she pulls off a thick coppery sweater, and rather than return it to the room,*

he pulls it over my head. Even though it looked like a normal sweater on her, once it is on me it seems to grow down to my ankles, so that I am completely covered and warm.

The joining of the clothing with the house suggests union and interconnection: Sayyid is a part of the tree. And the dreamer too receives such clothing, as if she too is now part of the tree.

Sayyid puts the kettle back on the stove, and begins sweeping the room, starting at the door and slowly spiraling in toward the center. "Watch," she says, "and see what you find." I watch him sweeping and at first don't see anything different, but then I realize that clouds of dirt from the floor are gathering as clouds in the room. Instantly I am gone—the room disappears and I am unable to move or see, though I still feel warm.

Slowly I begin to discern small bits of light, which I realize are stars. Next I feel that something is tickling me, and somehow I know that the night breezes are blowing across grass that is growing out of my body. Even though I am completely immobile, the stars are slowly crossing the sky, making me feel that I am the one moving. I am the one moving. As soon as I realize that I am the tree, I am thrown back into the room, where Sayyid has stopped sweeping. She wraps her arms around me, and I sob into his shoulder.

The shock of discovering the almost inconceivable truth that *she is the Tree* catapults Clare back into her body, where she sobs in Sayyid's arms, overcome. It is perhaps not an accident that in Arabic, the name Sayyid means "lord" or "master." Sayyid is a manifestation of the "master Tree," gently helping Clare toward the truth that she is part of all of This. Our dreams make us aware of the intricate web of Being in ways we often can't know when we are awake. This Tree within which the nebulae swirl is a profound image of the Presence that is Place. Clare writes that this "moving and powerful" dream has stayed with her for many years. It now stays with me as well.

WATER: THE GREAT DEEP

> This is the kind of water you can breathe, I thought. Perhaps there is just a secret to breathing water, something that everyone could do, if only they knew . . . The second thing I thought was that I knew everything . . . Ocean flowed inside me, and it filled the whole universe.
>
> —Neil Gaiman[9]

Scholar Marie Fernandes, commenting on Jung's view of water, wrote: "The river as symbol embodies the flow of life."[10] We might revise this by saying that water *is* life. Our bodies are mostly water. The Lakota say: *mni wiconi*, water is life. The Bible calls flowing water *mayyim chayyim*—living water. In Genesis, the Great Deep, the *tehom*, is the first companion of the Divine. Author Kai EL' Zabar says: "All life passes through water."[11]

In our dreams, water serves as a portal to the depths of the dream. Along the way, water often offers us the gift of immersion: the feeling of being entirely surrounded by the tangible ineffable. In the biblical imagination, the Great Deep is where the forces of pre-creation still dwell—where we can encounter something wilder, older, and more fluid than our human-ordered lives.

Water, which flows as one continuous entity, suggests the energetic flow of being. When we come to the Great Deep as a form of the underground temple, we frequently have a desire to immerse in it, even if it seems dangerous. Consider this dream, offered by a man I'll call Alan:

> *I am standing at the sliding back door of the house where I grew up in Connecticut, looking at the pond. Suddenly the water erupts over the banks and begins to flow toward a nearby stream with enormous force. I am shocked by its power.*
>
> *Then I look across the field. A thirty-foot wall of water is coming out of the woods and rushing toward the house. I tell everyone to get upstairs. I think they might survive up there. I start up the stairs to go with them, but turn around. I realize I don't want to avoid the water. It strikes me that this is what I truly want. I want to be with the water. The other people are afraid, and think the water is dangerous, but I just want to be taken by it.*
>
> *In a few seconds, the water is swirling around the house. I am back by the sliding glass door, and open it to let the water in. Somehow the idea that I might drown does not concern me. All I want is to be immersed in the water and carried away by the flood. Then I am floating away between the house and the barn. I don't know what happens to the people who went upstairs.*

The water that carries Alan away does not frighten him because it is part of him, and he is part of it. It is showing him he is one with the rest of Being. Alan knows not to run away from the water. He has a good "sense of direction" in this dream, orienting toward rather than away from the Presence, even if it is overwhelming and scary. Alan is demonstrating a good practice for dreams and waking life: choosing to go where the life is, where the movement is—to be motivated by love and desire rather than fear.[12] Elemental dream portals, because they draw us in with their immense energies and powers, help us approach what scares or overwhelms us—and therefore allow us to touch the Presence.

THE GREAT DEEP AS TEMPLE

In an ancient Sumerian myth, the world is made from the body of Tiamat, goddess of the depths of the sea.[13] In Genesis, the divine spirit—*ruach Elohim*, a feminine term—hovers over the *tehom* or primordial deep.[14] And in the Talmud, the channels dug beneath the Temple go down into the deep.[15] The depths of the ocean convey unfathomable power, and are often associated with the feminine. In the Zohar, one of the names for the Presence is *Yam*, sea. This feminine depth is one of the elemental portals we may encounter in dreams.

A rabbi friend, Leon, once dreamed a dream of the Great Deep, a dream he shared with me because I was in it. This dream, which alludes to a primordial feminine ocean-power, has been a great teacher of mine. He related it to me like this:

> *There are dozens of women gathered in a space that is between indoors and outdoors. You are sitting at an electric keyboard and beginning to play music that sounds like a harpsichord. At first, everyone stands about, a little unsure, and then three women start dancing—two who*

know the steps and one who doesn't know as
well, but is clearly delighted to learn, and hap-
py enough to skip and jump when she doesn't
know. Then all the women start dancing, wear-
ing rich, glorious dresses and headscarves.

I wonder if you might need a microphone, but
there is something about the combination of
the harpsichord with your voice that seems an
important balance to maintain. And then the
women become many, many women, and the
circle of the dancing becomes the currents of
the ocean—so that many other people who are
there have to move the continents into the cen-
ter of the dancing so that there will be room for
the waters to move as they need. The music
swells to fill the entire world, and everyone is
singing.

The women who join the dance seem to embody the diversity of life, moving together in colorful patterns. Yet they also seem like priestesses wildly dancing to the music of the depths. As the dreamer watches, the women multiply until the dance becomes an ocean, and the continents now must move to accommodate the flow of music and movement. The women are an embodiment of Sea-as-Presence—a multiplicitous but unified Being that touches all shores and fills all life with vitality.

This dream reminds me of an extraordinary vision in the Zohar, in which a sage is conversing with divine messengers who convey to him the secrets of the hidden worlds. They tell him that at the hour of dawn, "the Temple arises from the Deep, and the Holy One places it in the Great Sea, and its light illuminates the sky."[16] This Temple of the Deep is a portal into Presence. In our dreams, the

Deep may allow us to immerse in its elemental power and to join in its enchanting music.

AIR: THE STORM WIND

> What tongue does the wind talk?
> What nationality is a storm?
> —Ray Bradbury[17]

Elemental portals can help us transcend human concepts and let go into what is much greater than us. In the Bible, Psalm 29 depicts a worshipper bowing down to God in the glory of the Temple. Yet immediately after this reverent and serene image, the psalm turns to a God who is a terrifying thunderstorm: "The voice of God breaks cedars! The voice of God kindles flame! The voice of God convulses the deer!" The psalm moves back and forth between God resting in the Temple and God moving in the wilderness amid wind, thunder, and lightning. It becomes clear by the end of the psalm that the storm wind in the wilderness is itself the Presence in the Temple. The elemental world outside our doors is the real holy Place. Our human shrines are only an attempt to depict the primordial power of that Presence in all its glory.

Wind is the invisible force of the Creator. The kabbalists thus associate it with the realm of thought, and the world of the imagination—the unseen powers that inspire our creativity and govern our will. But wind is both a life-giving and a destructive force. In Genesis 2, God breathes life into Adam and creates a living being. In Psalm 29 the wind devastates the forest. In my dream experience, the forces of air often invite surrender to the blast of a greater Power—a yielding that makes it possible for us to release into something beyond ourselves.

A while ago, I had a dream that could have been an illustration of Psalm 29:

I am in an auditorium at a conference with people from the seminary that ordained me. It is the Sabbath. I have been invited to facilitate an earth-honoring ritual. The chancellor comes up to me and says: "They won't do it." I believe he means the group who has gathered to pray will think that what I am doing is wrong, and will refuse to do it. I tell him that I know these people and my ritual will be meaningful to the group. He looks disgusted and says: "We can discuss your history later." He wants to talk more, but I tell him I have to get my prayer shawl because the ritual is about to begin, and he is wasting the community's time. I'm angry at him, and I can see that he's angry at me.

I leave the room so I can prepare for my ritual: a ceremony honoring the four elements. I am having trouble thinking of how to embody each element. One of my friends is there, and she suggests using bells to embody air. I say: "No, it's Shabbat; they won't want to use instruments." She says, "We'll just use our breath," and I say, "Exactly." I imagine us blowing on water in copper bowls. I think that the air could represent Torah, but I'm tired and can't figure it all out. I feel disoriented.

Then my friend and I go outside. We are in a wide field, and a wild windstorm is approaching. Trees are whipping back and forth and falling over. One huge tree falls very near us. We run back to the main auditorium to protect ourselves. I'm walking into the ritual room and then I wake up.

This dream communicates my fear of being ostracized from my spiritual community. While there are many Jewish sources that see the earth as infused with divinity, there is a perception among some Jews that nature-focused ritual and practice is theologically worrisome. How to understand God's presence in nature is an old controversy among Jewish thinkers: the Chasidic masters saw nature as infused with God, while rationalist philosophers like Maimonides saw God as completely outside the natural world. The first part of the dream depicts my ritual as a point of contention—a way of staking out a position on this ancient question.

As my friend and I plan the ritual honoring the four elements, I'm feeling off-center, as if I need to defend my Jewish credentials to the hostile chancellor. I'm anxious for the ceremony to go well and please everyone. When my friend suggests that we just use our breath, this teaches me that attention to breath deepens our consciousness and helps us be more present in our experience. Breath is a portal to Presence. I am receiving the wisdom of the Presence: "Just breathe."

But I don't "just breathe." In the dream, I'm trying to symbolize Torah, the Genesis story, and so on, but such abstract "symbolizing" isn't what I should be doing. Instead of letting go into the Power I am trying to honor, I'm staying safe in my head, addressing the voice that thinks nothing I do is legitimate. This isn't helping me be present—I can't be with what is while I am arguing with someone inside my mind.

But then, the landscape changes, and the elements cut right through my theological issues, bringing me into a deeper sense of Place and Presence. Suddenly, we are outside in a field, and there is a massive windstorm knocking down trees, one of which almost falls on me and my ritual partner. This is not a symbolic construct of wind but the real Wind: the exact elemental power I wanted to invoke. This is indeed the kind of wind that swept over the face of the water at the dawn of creation—the *ruach Elohim*, the spirit-wind of God. This wind is not a symbol at all, but a portal to genuine Presence. Its voice, like the voice of the storm wind in Psalm 29, is calling me into a deeper sense of Being.

In the face of this mighty wind, religious conflicts within my little tribe are no longer relevant. My friend and I flee before the wind, and then I find myself at the door of the ritual space. The wind has shown me how to surrender to its immense power. Maybe now I am ready to create a ritual that embodies the presence of the wind as I feel and know it.

This dream teaches me how to open beyond what I already know, how to let go into mystery, how to do my ritual work with a fuller and wilder sense of the Being I am addressing. The elemental power of the windstorm allows me to lean into what is unfolding in front of me, rather than getting carried away by what is going on inside of me.

RIDING THE WIND

Joseph, whom we met in Chapter Two, dreamed of not only fleeing before the wind but being carried away by it, or even becoming it:

> I enter a house through the front door. Downstairs, there is a room with walls of dirt and a ceiling of roots. Upstairs, there is a room with a floor of grass and a ceiling of sky. A brook winds across the floor, and a small bridge spans it.
>
> I am met at the bridge by a being made of autumn leaves—not a solid figure covered with leaves, but a swirling cloud of wind-blown leaves in the rough shape of a man. This being escorts me back outside. The path outside the house leads toward a far horizon. A wind rises up behind me, and I am carried away toward the horizon as a flurry of leaves and butterflies.

"I remember that I came away from the dream with a profound sense of having encountered *Something*," Joseph told me. "My sense of the autumn-leaf man now is of a nurturing embrace, and of the transformative power of letting go." The wind's elemental power is a portal allowing Joseph to release his preconceptions and become his true self: a gathering of molecules in vibrant connection with the cosmos.

Dreams of the Wind may ask us to give in to the spirit moving invisibly but powerfully within. When we do, we let movement, newness, and change into our lives. As Toni Morrison wrote: "If you surrendered to the air, you could *ride* it."[18]

FIRE: THE ORCHARD OF LIGHT

> An angel appeared to him in a blazing fire out of a bush . . . "Remove your shoes from your feet, for the place on which you stand is holy ground."
> —Exodus[19]

In his vision of the Divine, Moses encounters a burning bush in the middle of the wilderness. The mother of Samson sees an angel rise up to heaven in fire. In Exodus, God leads the Israelites out of Egypt by appearing as a pillar of fire. When the portable shrine called the Tabernacle is set up for the first time, the Presence consumes the people's offerings in fire.[20] Fire, the element of the soul, is the element closest to the transcendent Divine according to the kabbalah. Its presence in a dream suggests the power of the spirit manifesting itself in tangible form.

Sharon, a yoga professor, shared with me a lucid dream in which she encountered a tree of fire:

> *I am walking, amazed, through an orchard*
> *full of cherry trees with pink and white flow-*
> *ers blooming. Then I turn around and see a*
> *night sky, where another tree, which seems to*
> *be made of fire or sparks, appears. It looks like*
> *a camera-film burning, as if the tree is drawing*
> *itself by burning the night sky all around. It*
> *looks like some sort of a "master tree."*

Throughout history, the orchard has appeared as one of the most potent and poetic expressions of the Tree of Life. The kabbalists call the Shekhinah, the Divine Presence, a beautiful name: the Holy Apple Orchard. She is the garden, the Place, in which souls are planted.[21] Avalon, the island of British myth, is associated with orchards, and the Norse goddess Idunna grows apples of immortality in her orchard. Hsi Wang Mu, Queen of the West, tends the orchard of the peaches of immortality in China. An orchard, as anyone who has walked through one in the spring can attest, is a place of wonder. It feels otherworldly, and this is perhaps why in all of these traditions, the otherworld looks like an orchard.

Surrounded by the pink and white flowers of the orchard, Sharon sees a tree of fire against the night sky. This image reminds us of the *menorah*, the sacred lamp shaped like a tree, with its "branches" and "blossoms." It also evokes the kabbalistic philosophy of Isaac Luria, in which the world is composed of sparks of divine light, shrouded in shells that conceal their radiance.[22] When the shells shatter and scatter the sparks everywhere, each spark must be found, lifted up, and returned to the whole.

The tree of fire that Sharon sees "draws itself." It seems to self-generate out of the vast dark by burning the night sky. This suggests life arising out of the void. We might say that Sharon is walking through Eden and discovers the Tree of Life. In this dream, fire suggests the hidden worlds, the soul, and the light that streams through the cosmos. Sharon writes: "I cannot express the feeling it left me with in words. The dream made me feel as if I was able to touch my soul, or the Divine. I would have liked to stay in that orchard forever." Of course, we can't stay in Eden forever—we have to return to waking life. And yet we can return there again and again, through the portals in our dreams.

FINDING THE POWER
IN A DREAM PORTAL

How do we recognize the elemental portals in our dreams where we can dive past our everyday thoughts and feelings and come into contact with the Presence?

For starters, we can begin by noticing dream landscapes that hold unusual life, beauty, or strangeness. These might be obvious, like a massive conscious tree. Or they might be less obvious, like a bright blue vegetable in a supermarket. The way you know you've found an elemental portal is if its beauty or mystery insistently draws your attention.

As a way to illustrate how we might work with a portal dream, let's look at two dreams I dreamed one after the other on the same night.

Dream 1:

> *I'm in a remote area of Coney Island. There is a salt marsh there with lots of little inlets. Under the shallow water is bright green grass, long and flowing in the current. I wade into the water and am happy.*
>
> *Then friends come, and we all go to a swimming pool nearby. Eventually, we want to return to our bungalow. Halfway back, I realize I have forgotten my shoes and am wearing my daughter's flip-flops. I go back and get my shoes, but*

now I have forgotten the flip-flops and need to
go back for them.

Dream 2:

> *I am at the place where I teach. The building*
> *has many floors. I am on one floor having lunch*
> *and reading a good book. I look at my phone*
> *and see that I am late for class. I am worried*
> *about how angry the dean will be. I have trouble*
> *putting on my shoes and now I am even later.*
> *I rush up the stairs and see that all of my stu-*
> *dents are hanging out on the landing waiting for*
> *me. They follow me into the classroom and sit*
> *down. I say: "I feel like I've never been in this*
> *class before."*
>
> *My feet are hot and I take off my socks. I say,*
> *"These socks are too hot for normal human*
> *people." I get ready to teach. I decide I am go-*
> *ing to teach my dream about the bright green*
> *grass under the water.*

What I remember most vividly about these dreams is the water with the long green grass. This is the portal in the dream, the doorway to Place and Presence. I know it by the brightness of the green. I also know it by the joy that I feel.

When I reflect on that moment in the dream when I approach the water and gaze down into the slowly undulating grass, what I want most is to put my feet in the flowing water and feel the softness of the grass on my toes. The rest of the dream points me back to that desire. Throughout the dream, I keep forgetting my shoes, which suggests my desire to be barefoot, to connect to the earth and its powerful elemental energy. My shoelessness is reminiscent of the moment when God says to Moses, "Take off your shoes, for the place where you are standing is holy ground."[23] In the dream, I think that I should "go back" for my shoes, and yet I keep forgetting them, which suggests that the loss of my shoes—the removal of the barriers between me and the world—is what needs to happen.

Notably, the second dream is a commentary on the first dream, and the Talmud says that a dream that is interpreted within a dream is always fulfilled.[24] In the second dream, I am finding pleasure in lunch and a good book when I realize I'm late for class. I once again have trouble with my shoes and socks: I still want to be barefoot, to be a "normal human person" at home in my physical body. Within the dream, I decide I want to teach about the dream of the grass. Even while still dreaming, I am returning to that elemental moment, the portal through which I enter into deeper communion with Presence. When I am connected that way, everything feels new and dynamic, as if I've never been there before.

In waking life, I know the dream is saying that I should sometimes leave my shoes behind. The dream is reminding me that I need to directly connect to the earth in order to be grounded, whole, and healthy. I need to try as often as I can to walk outside barefoot.

Since that dream, when I become anxious and overwhelmed, I sometimes try to remember the long grass flowing in the water. This cool, fluid image soothes me and shifts my consciousness. And the image reminds me of a biological fact about dreams: when we enter deep sleep, the brain pushes fluid through its cells to clean them. When we don't get enough sleep, this cleaning process happens imperfectly, and this can eventually harm the brain.[25] Sometimes, when I really need a long, deep sleep that cleanses my brain, I imagine my brain cells as the flowing green grasses, with the water flowing through and cleaning them.

My desire to get my shoes, to be socially acceptable, is an obstacle to my being present in the moment. When I compare my anxiety in much of the dream to my joy near the bright green grass, I can see where I would rather be. Your dream, too, may show you a place, element, relationship, or activity where you find joy. Or, your dream may show you where you feel distant and disconnected. The dream itself gives you clues as to how to navigate the labyrinth and find the portal.

FULL IMMERSION:
BRINGING THE DREAM INTO THE
WAKING WORLD

Here's another way of working with a dream in which water serves as a portal into deeper Presence. In this dream, Paul, a philosopher and retired civil servant, comes to the edge of some cold, deep water but does not want to get in:

> *Standing on a dock, I accidentally drop an expensive snorkel mask into the water and it sinks to the bottom. The water is very dark and deep. When I look down and see the mask, I feel it doesn't belong to me, and I need to retrieve it so as to return it to its owner. Yet I am afraid that going so deep might harm me because of the water pressure.*
>
> *I go inside to ask my father if I may borrow a boat to go retrieve the mask. I ask hesitantly because I fear my father won't lend me the boat. My father doesn't respond, but a woman who is with my father says that of course I can take the boat.*

I invited Paul to revisit the dream in his mind. He noted that anticipating the shock of the cold water was unpleasant, and agreed that his reluctance to retrieve the mask was about his fear of the water. We discussed Paul's father and the mysterious woman who lends Paul the boat. Paul noted his distance from his father in the dream and in real life, and also reflected on the woman's unexpected kindness. This unfamiliar woman clearly was encouraging him to return to the water.

We kept coming back to the moment of looking into the dark, cold water with foreboding. In that moment, it didn't seem that what Paul needed was a boat. A boat wouldn't help him get the mask. A snorkel mask is meant for breathing underwater, and this suggested to me that Paul was meant to immerse: the dark water was the portal that summoned Paul deeper. When Paul said that the mask he dropped "does not belong to me," I felt that the mask was itself part of the deep, a place which cannot belong to any human being, but to which we in fact belong.

In response to the dream, I took an intuitive leap and asked Paul to find a body of water to jump into in waking life. Paul gamely agreed. He considered a local indoor swimming pool but that didn't seem right. Finally, on a hike in the Rocky Mountains, he found a cold stream to immerse in. The water was icy and he felt the same resistance he had felt in the dream. He persisted, and jumped in. He was surprised by what a good experience it was. He later told me:

> The healing thing about it was that being in the water cleared my mind completely of rumination. It was a joining of my sentient body with the water. There was no sense of otherness.

Paul expresses the goal of elemental dreaming perfectly: "A joining of my sentient body with the water." This joining, he said, had a "friendly feeling." This exercise may prepare him to take more "leaps" of this kind in other areas of his life. In the water, Paul found his elemental portal to the Place of deeper Presence.

Paul later thanked me for the experience, which he thought he would not have tried without the dream. He added: "What's been meaningful is this gap between rumination and the 'réalité rugueuse,'[26] the actual, wrinkled texture of reality." In other words, fear of the water is scarier than the water itself.

An elemental portal tends to have a sense of mystery to it—maybe a moment of striking beauty (the grass), or of raw terror (the dark water). If you think you have encountered such a portal, pay careful attention to what you experienced and how it made you feel. See if you can sit with the Presence at the heart of the dream. Don't try to "solve" it. Just honor the feeling.

Later, if you want to explore further, you can find a quiet moment to reenter the dream in your imagination: What elements, structures, or land features are around you, and how do you feel about them? What people or entities do you meet and how do you feel about them? Do you have a sense of holiness, awe, or fascination at any point in the dream? Is there any place or encounter that makes you want to linger, or run away? If so, go deeper into that place or encounter. What is its power? What emotion, or what wisdom, does it bring up for you?

You can also use journaling and art-making to plumb your dream's images more deeply. For example, you can write in the voice of the elemental entity from your dream. That entity—the Tree of Life, Storm Wind, etc.—may tell you why it has appeared to you, what it needs you to know, and what its gifts are. If you want, you can paint or draw the images, meditate on them, or write poems or stories about them. For example, I know people who have received a song in a dream, and who regularly sing that song.

Some of my dream clients like to build a "dream altar," a sacred space that recalls a powerful dream and brings its images into waking life. You can place elements from your dream in such a sacred space. To honor my grass dream, for example, I might use a bowl with floating grasses or flowers. For a fire dream, I might use a candle.

Dreams often show us the elements we are lacking in our lives, so we can take the dream as a "prescription" for what we need most. You can use the method Paul and I used and seek out in waking life the elements that appeared to you in the dream. If you saw a forest, go hike in the forest. If you immersed in water, go for a swim. If you dreamed of being barefoot, go barefoot! While you're outside in the elements, you can ask the natural world what it's trying to tell you, or what healing it has to offer. Listen all around you for the answer.

Rabbi Nachman of Breslov, an eighteenth-century mystic thinker (1772–1810), had a similar practice. He prayed: "May it be my custom to go outdoors each day among the trees and grasses and all growing things, and there may I be alone, and enter into prayer, to talk with the One to whom I belong. May I express there everything in my heart, and may all the foliage of the field, all grasses, trees, and plants, awake at my coming, to infuse the powers of their life into the words of my prayer."[27]

Amen!

CHAPTER 4

Guardians of the Dream Temple

Our most immediate experience of things … is necessarily an experience of reciprocal encounter.
   —David Abram[1]

Something elemental … hints at the unfathomable, creating a world where divine love may, despite our pain, prevail.
   —Avivah Gottlieb Zornberg[2]

The Tree of Life, the Great Deep, and the Storm Wind are not the only beings we encounter within dreams. We also meet entities that relate to us much more personally, bringing us messages, healing, and sacred encounter. The dream temple has guardians, healers, and wise teachers who help us to connect to the temple's deeper reality. In other words, the Place is often tended by a Presence. (We've already encountered such beings: Sayyid, whom we found tending the Tree of Life in Chapter Three, is one example.) When Jacob sees in his dream the ladder between heaven and earth, and suddenly finds God standing next to him, he is experiencing a guardian at the gateway to his dream temple. Indeed, upon waking he marvels: "This is none other than God's house, and this is the gate to heaven."[3]

The understanding that dream characters are messengers has a long history. Medieval Jewish tradition describes the *maggid* or "one who tells": a spirit entity that communicates with human beings and shares hidden wisdom, sometimes through a dream. Joseph Caro, writer of the sixteenth-century law code called the Shulchan Arukh, had a *maggid* whom he identified with the Shekhinah, and who visited him in dreams and in waking visions.[4] The sixteenth-century kabbalist Isaac Luria called such dream messengers the "answering angels."[5]

We too may meet a *maggid* in our dreams: a person or entity who meets us at the portal to Being. We might see such entities as messengers of Presence, guiding us on our journey to repair self and world. These messengers, who hold elemental power yet also interact with us on a personal level, help us bridge the awe-inspiring cosmic Presence and our own human perceptions. Like Paracelsus, the fifteenth-century alchemist who used the term "elemental" to mean a being that embodied one of the four elements,[6] I too often use the term "elementals" to describe this kind of dream messenger. We might call these elementals emissaries of Being. They stand at the portals of our dreams, inviting us deeper.

In this chapter, we'll encounter some examples of these dream guardians and messengers. As you read, think about the beings you've met in your own dreams. It might be that you will now understand them in a different light.

THE GREAT BEAR

> I dream again and again of a giant bear that
> is in my house. It's not attacking me but it
> is so large that I am frightened . . . It's alive
> and rank and feral. Its great arms are around
> me and I think, "That's it, I'm going to be
> crushed." But the bear is gentle. The bear
> says: "Call on me and I'll show you what you
> need to be healed and what others need to be
> healed." The bear and I are joined heart to
> heart, heart-center to heart-center. And since
> then I've been connected to the bear.
> —Robert Moss[7]

When I first began to ask people to tell me their dreams, I noticed that my friends (who lived in suburban houses and urban apartments, far from the woods) kept dreaming about bears—and I wondered why. As I asked more friends, and encountered more bear dreams, I discovered that the bear often appeared at a door, fence, or gateway. I began to see the bear as a guardian of the underground temple.

Simon took a dream class with me while training to be a cantor. This dream of the Great Bear that he shared with me is a passage into the underground temple, as well as a journey of memory, healing, and love.

> *I am standing beside the ruins of Old Boling-*
> *broke Castle in Lincolnshire, where I did an*

archaeological training dig in 1970. I am ex-
hausted; my neck, back, legs, and shoulders
ache, as they often did then. It is late in the
evening but the moon is bright enough to light
the way to my tent. I stop briefly at the water
pump to take a long drink and splash cold wa-
ter on my face and neck, which feels wonderful.

Then I walk to my tent, strip off my shoes and
boots, and crawl into my sleeping bag. Sud-
denly, the tent is shaking, and so is my body;
there's a deafening pounding. Afraid, I rush out
to see what's happening. The cattle in the ad-
jacent field are stampeding, circling in closer
and closer to the fencing that surrounds our
encampment. As I watch, a bull charges the
fence near me. I run away, and can feel small
stones cutting into my feet.

I am racing up the hill toward the keep when
I realize that the ground is collapsing beneath
me. I land on a slide of some kind, and end up
in a dark, narrow stone passage. I realize that I
must be in a deep portion of the Castle's base-
ment that has miraculously remained intact. It
is quiet but I feel safe.

As I walk the stone corridor, my eyesight and
hearing gradually improve as I become accus-
tomed to the dark and quiet. I realize it is not
silent here. I am certain there is sound that
is just beyond the limits of my hearing, and I
know I need to hear that sound.

I stop, turn, and place my palms against the wall. I feel the cold filling my palms and spreading along my arms. The sound is clearer now, pulsing mournfully within the walls. I relax my defenses, allowing the musical energy that flows through the wall to pass into and through me as well. There are psalms of praise and hymns of loss. They are difficult to parse but so infused with feeling as to be unmistakable in their meanings. I feel what the ancients felt, and am convulsed first in agony, then joy, until I can reach inside myself and hold my own emotions at a distance—while still loving them.

With the psalms still reverberating through my body, I let go of the stone. I hear the voices echoing dimly off the walls; they seem to be coming from far down the corridor. I follow them.

At the end of the corridor, I encounter an enormous black bear. I run to hug him. I know that it must be my father, who died when I was nine: it's identical to the carved black bear he brought home from Germany after the war. He engulfs me in his hairy arms, lifts me off the ground and smiles. "You found your way," he says. "You're learning to hear the music of the stones and touch them."

Then he steps aside. A flight of stairs emerges behind him. With a nod of the head he sends me on my way. I do not want to go. I hang on tightly and cry. Then I awake.

In the dream, we meet two animal guardians: the bull and the bear. The fence where Simon encounters the charging bull seems to mark the boundary between the mundane, and a realm where the dreamer can find transformation. The bull suggests the wild and powerful Presence in the dream. As Simon proceeds deeper into the earth, the aliveness of the cosmos comes to him in the songs of the stone walls. As Simon listens, he feels "what the ancients felt": the joy and sorrow of being alive. The dream is introducing him to the Place that is Presence—to the animate sacred world.

Here, at this portal to Presence, Simon meets a bear he recognizes as a manifestation of his father, who lovingly praises him for his new wisdom. This affectionate bear connects to the human realm and also to the elemental forces of the earth. Through the bear guardian, the dream offers Simon the healing and release of embracing and being embraced by his father, combined with the joy of hearing the stones' song. Love and awe are thus seamlessly woven together.

In my mind, the music of the stones that the Great Bear guards is the music of life. We too may hear the music of the stones when we hike a mountain trail or pick up shells on the beach. We may hear it when we pray or meditate, or when we remember the beings who have walked this earth before us. We may hear it in the people we love. Such music is waiting for us in the forests and fields all around us. As Rabbi Nachman of Breslov once said, every blade of grass has a song.[8]

THE SEA SERPENT

> God created angels in the upper worlds, human beings in this world, and the Leviathan in the sea.
> —Zohar[9]

In Genesis 1:21, God creates the monsters of the deep sea during the fifth day of creation. In Psalm 104, God speaks of creating Leviathan, the great sea serpent. In the Talmud, Leviathan is said to be the playmate of God.[10] The creatures of the deep have been part of the human imagination for centuries. As I collected dreams for this book, I discovered that the underground temple can be an underwater temple, and that just as we may encounter an animal at the portal to the temple of the earth, we may encounter a sea creature at the portal to the temple of water. Water creatures beckon us to fully immerse in the world of the dream.

I powerfully encountered such a guardian when my daughter was six. Already then she gravitated to water: baths, swimming pools, rivers, the ocean. She reported to me this dream:

> *I have a party with my friends. Mama shows us a secret passage to another world through a dot on a piece of paper. I already know about that passage because I have seen it in another dream. In that other world, I have to win a boyfriend in a pinball game. My boyfriend is invisible and only I can see him. He is beautifully dressed. I choose a dark gold ruffled dress for myself and we all go to a dance.*
>
> *Then the boyfriend leaves to go home and my friends and I go with Mama to another place with a giant sea serpent. I remember having visited him in another dream where I slept in his arms. At first the sea serpent does not know us and we have to answer questions: it is a test. When we get the questions right, he remembers us. He picks me up, and my friends are afraid he will eat me. Instead, I go to sleep in his arms.*

The girl and her friends embark on a quest to the "other world" via a dot on a piece of paper. A single mark, the most basic component of human written language, becomes the doorway to the deeper temple. This is the nature of dream language: the images are doorways to something deeper. The fairy-tale nature of the dream—the invisible prince-like boyfriend, the beautiful dress—suggests a wondrous place, a world in which the little girl can grow into her full self. But the core of the dream is the sea serpent, the elemental being.

The dreamer, through the voices of her friends, expresses a fear that the sea serpent will eat her, yet she remains calm and drawn to it. I have found this double-edged feeling of fear and awe to be typical of encounters with dream guardians. The guardians who keep the hidden temple can be frightening as well as kind. We cannot control or define them with the conscious mind. They are manifestations of something wild and unpredictable. Yet they also are guides. The sea serpent in the dream is loving and gentle, and he "remembers" the dreamer—he knows she is innately part of his world.

The biblical myth of Leviathan, the Japanese tale of Ryujin the sea dragon, the world-circling Norse sea serpent Jörmungandr—all these sea monsters arise from the fathomless deep: the primordial ocean from which life emerged, but which remains unfathomable to us. The appearance of such a creature in my daughter's dream lets her know that she has come to a portal where she may fully immerse in Being, and that she is firmly held and fully loved while she does so. Indeed, her surrendering to sleep in the sea serpent's arms shows his affection for her, and may also mean that he is taking her one level deeper into the dreamworld, into a dream within a dream.

It is one thing to read about dragons and
another to meet them.
—Ursula K. Le Guin[11]

The experience of contact with an elemental dream guide, and the
portal that guide tends, can be a life-altering experience. The witness of such a dream guardian can alter our self-understanding.
When I was twenty, I encountered a dragon in my dreams, who
taught me that wonder and appreciation for the profound beauty
of creation are at the core of my life.

> As I emerge from a forest path, I find before me
> a dusty bridge over a river or canyon. It is a
> simple bridge, made of rough wooden slats, with
> logs sunk into the earth to anchor it. Across the
> bridge is an immense building with tall glass
> windows. It looks like a palace, though it does
> not rise very high off the ground. It is as if much
> of the building is underground. I am curious
> and also a little afraid. I leave the forest and
> cross the bridge.
>
> As I cross, I see to my right a low structure
> like a stable. Inside are several dragons. They
> have huge wings and thick ridges on their
> backs. One of them rises to meet me, and I
> climb onto its back. I can't see it very well, but
> I can feel how big it is. The dragon takes off and
> flies through an open door into the immense
> palace-like building. I am exhilarated by the
> sensation of flight.

I can see that the building is indeed partly underground, and much larger and taller inside than it looked from the outside. Inside the massive edifice are miles of magnificent gardens, full of impossibly bright-colored flowers in every hue. Even though the gardens are underground, the glass windows let in bright sunlight.

The dragon flies me over these gardens, spinning several times so that I get a 360-degree view. Every section of the garden is different from the one before, and every view is gorgeous. Enchanted by the beauty, I want the dragon to keep flying and flying. I discover that I can use my mind to direct the dragon to any part of the garden I want to see.

As we circle over the gardens, I become aware that I am dreaming and that I am beginning to wake. With all my might, I try not to wake up, but as the dragon whirls above the garden and more and more kinds of flowers appear, I feel myself waking.

I can remember and relive this dream as if it was yesterday. From the moment I climbed onto the dragon, it was as if we were one creature. Why do I feel this strong kinship with the dragon? The dragon's appearance and its merging with me in flight lets me know something about myself: my own fiery spark within, my desire to soar, to discover new worlds. This dream gave me a sense of my own power to journey, to experience joy and awe—a sense that has never left me. The wonder remains, even now, thirty years later. After all these years, I am still finding the dragon in myself.

You too may have had a dream where you met a guardian of the Place. Your guardian might not be a bear or a sea serpent or a dragon. It might be a bird or a deer or a snake or any creature that appears at a moment when the dream goes deeper. When we meet a guardian, particularly an elemental, it is a sign we are ready for that deeper journey. We have to watch our dreams carefully to find the portals to our temple—and to find our guides along the way.

CONNECTING WITH
A DREAM GUARDIAN

When we meet dream guardians, how can we identify them and open ourselves to their gifts, power, and love? How can we let these elementals lead us to the elemental in ourselves? In this section, we'll consider how we can find our guardians and receive their messages.

As an example, we will work with a dream offered by one of my clients, Nessa, a rabbinical student and kohenet. In one of our sessions together, we explored the setting, narrative, and characters present in this dream, in order to locate a dream guardian and integrate their wisdom. During this process, we were able to identify moments of blockage by reentering the images and feelings of the dream, and as a result we uncovered a profound opportunity for liberation and opening.[12]

In the dream, Nessa is walking through the city where she lived in childhood. She hates the new look of the city: less green and more concrete. Later in the dream, she's trying to run an errand and gets on the wrong bus, which takes her someplace she doesn't expect:

> *I run into a friend, who is a musician and edu-*
> *cator. He tells me that I should get on the #13*
> *bus, but it takes me in the wrong direction, past*

grassy fields and white marble statues of Athena and Artemis. Then we go into a tunnel. The bus driver starts singing. His voice is beautiful. He's like a gospel choir soloist, with a deep, full, earthy voice. He says he wanted to wait until we got into the tunnel because the sound is better in there.

A few people join in with the driver, and soon the whole bus is joyfully harmonizing. I'm nervous, not sure if my voice belongs in the mix, but then I join in with a quiet, tentative "aaaaah" note. I think far too late that maybe I should record the singing on my phone, but I can't find it. Have I lost it? It was just in my pocket! I only find it again after the singing. It has been in my jacket pocket all along.

In the beginning of this dream, Nessa wanders through a mundane landscape full of concrete until her friend, a musician, sends her to the Number Thirteen bus. Thirteen recalls the thirteen moons of the year, and is a sacred number to the Goddess in some traditions. It is clear this is no ordinary bus. As the Number Thirteen bus heads for greener landscapes, dotted with images of ancient goddesses, we can feel ourselves going deeper.

When I ask Nessa what she feels about the bus, she says: "It's a soul bus, a bus that's bound for glory." The "soul bus" is bringing her where she needs to go: deep under the earth, into the underground temple.

Deep inside a tunnel, the driver begins to sing in his "earthy" voice, joined by the other passengers. This song is the moment of beauty in the dream that indicates the dreamer has come to a portal, a place to go deeper. It is not an accident that this place is underground; we are once again under the conscious mind and embedded in the earth. And the bus driver is the guardian of this portal to Presence.

When I ask Nessa to feel what it is like to hear the song, she says: "I am in the presence of something powerful and connected that I don't understand. I am in awe of it. I want to be a part of it but it's big and beautiful and terrifying, like the experience of the infinite." This is a perceptive knowing of the Presence, the elemental reality of Being.

In the dream, Nessa's response to the singing is to want to sing too—and then to feel that her voice isn't good enough. She becomes distracted by her self-doubt and loses her sense of connection to the music. This self-deprecation seems like the blockage in the dream. When I ask about this, Nessa agrees that self-consciousness is an issue that's manifested in her life before. The dream, I suggest, has come to diagnose this blockage and help clear it. That Nessa finds her phone at the end of the dream suggests she has been able to "record"—remember—the song all along.

I ask Nessa to go back into the moment of making the *ahhh* sound. She makes the *ahhh* for me: a sad and tentative *ahhh*. When I ask how it feels, Nessa says: "It's pretty vulnerable. There's so much of me that is scared that I am not making the right sound. My voice doesn't really belong with all these people. I wish I could make strong harmonizing notes with all the other people. This feels sad and frustrating."

I ask Nessa to become her dream again, but this time sing a full *ahhh* with the driver and the passengers, without worrying about how it sounds. She sings again. This sound is completely different than the first: a full, loud, long note. Nessa feels in her power and in her joy. I can tell by the smile that something is different. "I feel like a channel," she says. Nessa is discovering her song—the elemental power of air within her own body.

I ask Nessa to make the *ahhh* sound or imagine it whenever she feels doubt about sharing the fullness of her voice. I invite her to see the bus driver as a companion—to imagine him listening carefully to her song and supporting her in singing. I ask her what the bus driver is saying to her, and she replies: "If you think you have something to sing, you should sing it. Don't listen to the voices that tear you down. Listen to me."

The next time I see Nessa, her voice has become more confident and powerful. Two years later, she sings a solo at a bonfire ritual that stuns the whole community with its beauty. The bus driver who brought her into the tunnel of song has invited her into the power of her voice.

When you wake up and reflect on a dream, try to remember if you can identify a person, animal, or entity who might be a guardian or guide, showing you how to connect with a dream portal. Try to notice: Whom do you trust in the dream? From whom do you receive help, love, or support? At moments when there is deep beauty, awe, confusion, or constriction, is there someone there who helps or directs you? What characters connect you to more-than-human energies?

Ask yourself: Who is my dream guide? Is there a temple or garden or underwater realm to which this guide is leading me? Where else might this guide take me if I let them?

Often, as in the dreams in this chapter, the dream guardian or guide offers a loving presence, deeply supporting the dreamer. How does your dream guide show you love and support? What might be different in your life if you accepted this love? Or, if your dream guide is scary, what are they trying to get you to notice or understand?

What does your dream guardian say or do? Do you get any clue, from where they are or what they say or do, as to what your gifts or blockages might currently be? Do you notice any advice about how to apply the dream in your waking life?

If you're unsure, you can ask a friend or other trusted person for help in figuring out who the guardian is and what their message might be. Or you can use journaling to ask the guardian what their message is: write a letter to the dream character asking your questions, and then write their letter back to you! Using your imagination in this way may give you insight into the dream's deeper meaning.

You can also revisit the dream scene in your mind's eye, freeze the dream, and ask one of the characters a question. Some questions to ask might be: What is the next step of my journey? Where can I find the support I need to take that step? What is the healing I need? Whom should I seek out for connection? What sacred practices do I need at this time? Which elements do I need to connect with?

If you have a particularly powerful experience with a dream guardian, that's a gift and a cause for gratitude. We can always choose to come back to our most powerful dream guardians in prayer or meditation, or whenever we want to connect to Being—just as Nessa asked the bus driver for support when she sang.

Remember: a dream guide or guardian doesn't have to have a message that can be conveyed in words. We can simply be with them and feel their Presence.

If you comb through your dream and the message or the messenger isn't immediately clear, you can practice what the sages of the Talmud say that Jacob practiced upon hearing Joseph's dreams: you can wait to see how the dream will be fulfilled. "Rabbi Levi said: one should await fulfillment of a good dream for up to twenty-two years."[13] Sometimes what starts out as opaque becomes clear over time.

Remember that dream guardians shift from dream to dream. You might see a particular guide or guardian again, or you might see a different being in the next dream, with a new way of showing you how to find the portal into Presence.

CHAPTER 5

Healing in Our Dreams

The dreams know exactly what we need, how we need it, and the way to deliver that message that is so unique and personal for us.

—Mary Jo Heyen[1]

Once we go through the dream portal, encounter the sacred places, and meet the dream guides, what happens then? My experience is that the temple in our dreams is not just a place for visiting; it is a place of healing. We go there to connect but also to transform. The eighteenth-century Chasidic rebbe Reb Zusya once said that "even sleep has a purpose. One who wishes to progress [spiritually] must put aside their life-work in order to receive a new spirit. . . . This is the secret of sleep."[2] Sleep allows us to enter a transformative space where we can find renewal, and even revelation.

Cultures that value dreaming have long known that dreams can heal. For example, the Haudenosaunee (Iroquois) people believe dreams can "help to cure disease, as well as disorders of the mind . . . [caused by] resentments and unmet needs and desires."[3] Jewish folk tradition also speaks of healing dreams. Such healing may relate to physical ailments, emotional malaise, spiritual blockages, or societal harm.

In the kabbalah, a healing is often called a *tikkun*, a fixing, a repair. The Chasidic master Rebbe Nachman of Breslov said: "Each person must see themselves as if the world was created for them. And, since the world was created for me, I must at all times be searching for the healing (*tikkun*) that is possible in the world."[4] So too in our dreams, we may receive the gift of healing for ourselves or others.

Years ago, after a dream circle, a woman approached me and told me the following story. Her husband's brother, who was dead, came to her in a dream. He told her that her husband had an undiagnosed heart condition, and was in danger of dying. In the morning, she took her husband to a cardiologist, who said that her husband was fine. But the woman trusted her dream and insisted on a second opinion. The second doctor diagnosed an immense artery blockage and rushed the woman's husband into surgery. "Your husband was days from dying," the doctor told the woman. Over the years, I have heard many stories like this. The healing we can receive from the dreamworld is nothing short of miraculous.

Our next four chapters will deal with the different levels of healing that can take place within the heart of the dream.

THE APOTHECARY: DREAM MEDICINES

One of my most astonishing experiences with dream healing happened in a dream market. A market is a sacred, liminal place where one can receive something new. Novelist Lian Hearn writes: "There is a sort of magic going on at markets. Goods are bartered, one thing transformed into another."[5] Nam-lin Hur, analyzing the marketplace in early modern Japan, concurs: "Street markets were not purely places for trade . . . The first form of trade had a religious component: prospective traders first ritually offered their commodities to deities and then proceeded to deal with customers."[6] The dream market is thus a place where we may find the gifts we need for healing and transformation, as I did in this dream:

> *I'm in a big outdoor market, going from stall to stall. I come to a stall that sells herbs, and I want to buy the big jar of witch hazel sitting on the counter, to help me with the cracks on my feet. The jar is green, and appealing.*
>
> *A heavy woman in late middle age is serving customers. She reminds me of the nurse who helped my daughter when she was in the emergency room with asthma. The woman tells me that I ordered some candy last week and gives it to me: a jar of round glassy spheres. I no longer want the candy and put it on the ground. I see another jar of elderberry syrup and think*

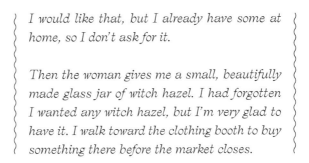

I would like that, but I already have some at home, so I don't ask for it.

Then the woman gives me a small, beautifully made glass jar of witch hazel. I had forgotten I wanted any witch hazel, but I'm very glad to have it. I walk toward the clothing booth to buy something there before the market closes.

When I woke, I thought "witch hazel" must be a reference to the archetypal Witch, the magic-worker who heals via plants and the energies of the earth. But then I realized the dream might have a more practical message, too.

At the time I had this dream, I was suffering from psoriasis. For ten years, there were itchy red patches on my feet, and nothing seemed to help. After this dream, I applied liquid witch hazel (a remedy no one else had suggested to me) to the rash, and it immediately stopped itching. A few weeks later, after many more applications of witch hazel, the rash was completely healed. Now, six years later, I still have no psoriasis on my feet. The dream accurately prescribed the literal medicine I needed.

Of course, not all dreams offer us medicine in such a literal way. But a dream may offer us a more subtle form of medicine. The important thing is to notice when the dream is presenting us with a prescription for some ailment or trouble that we may have. For example, in a recent dream of mine, I am a graduate student with teaching responsibilities, but am so busy writing a novel that I keep missing the class I am supposed to teach! The dream suggests that I feel pressured by responsibility and need more creative time in my life—and invites me to see what happens when I make that time. We don't need to regard dream healing as symbolic or esoteric. Often the dream is telling us something quite direct and practical that we can act upon in our waking lives.

VISITS FROM DREAM HEALERS

In some healing dreams, a healer arrives and does energetic work on our bodies. Years ago, Sheikh Dr. Ibrahim Baba Farajaje, a professor, queer theologian, and spiritual teacher with both Muslim and Jewish connections, was in the hospital with a life-threatening lung infection. He dozed, and in his dream, he saw an archangel reach into his chest and pull something out. The archangel communicated without words that all would be well, and that Farajaje had received this initiatory healing so that he could help others. The next day, all of the pathological tissue in his lungs had vanished.[7]

In other healing dreams, the dreamer may be offered a medicinal food. Wendy of New York City, who works in health-care media, describes a period twenty years ago in which she entered a deep depression. She endured, in her own words, "weeks of feeling dull, unavailable, dispirited: quiet suffering. I was in therapy but it wasn't helping me. I couldn't shake it." Then she had this dream:

> I am wandering alone in the desert. I do not feel depressed, worried, or scared. I come to a large canvas tent and walk inside. Inside the tent is an elephant. I walk around the elephant slowly. The elephant stays very still. Then I notice a man sitting on a big comfortable pillow in the corner. In front of him is a low table with a bowl on it.
>
> He gestures for me to sit down with him. I do. We don't speak. He lifts the bowl off the table and gestures, offering it to me. I ask him what it is. He says it is made from fava beans and is called ful mudammas. I eat it.

Undertorah

Ful mudammas is an Egyptian breakfast dish of fava beans and hummus, a Middle Eastern dish from an ancient recipe. Fava beans were one of the oldest domesticated legumes, and one of the most common protein sources in biblical ancient Israel. The food Wendy consumes is ancestral food, containing the centuries of relationship between humans and the earth. Not only this, but sitting and sharing food is a fundamental act of companionship and kindness. The sharing of food in the tent is a healing of human relationship, and beyond, since the elephant is from the more-than-human world.

The aftermath of the dream was immediate. Wendy reports: "This dream was shamanic. I was different. The entire next day, I felt a sense of not being in this world. My depression lifted." Dreams such as this offer, within the dream, an intervention in the dreamer's body that has immediate impact in waking life.

SWIMMING WITH DOLPHINS: DREAM-HEALING THROUGH WITNESS

In some dreams, the dream healer listens to us and knows our troubles, and that witnessing provides the healing we need. Such a dream can help us feel seen when we have been feeling isolated and alone. Isabelle, a kohenet who works on anti-oppression issues, shared this dream:

> *I am on a vacation, and I have to use the bathroom. So I leave a crowded cabin full of White people to find a toilet. I wind up in a low-roofed pavilion area where there are a lot of Black people. I give a guy I meet there a pair of sneakers, then sit down, tired.*
>
> *An expressive and vibrant young woman sits down with me. She has a message for me. She*

says: "Stay the path!" I am getting teary-eyed. I notice we are sitting on a tall green cliff. At the bottom of the cliff is a lake. I see dolphins and black-and-white whales.

At this point, an older Black woman arrives. She mumbles that the young one always creates a lot of noise to give messages, and shoos the young woman away. Somehow my daughter is with me, and I say, "She would love swimming with the dolphins," so the young woman takes her into the water. It turns out the young woman is a mermaid. I smile and touch her fin. Another young girl appears, and when I ask about my daughter, she says: "She is by the edge of the water." We giggle that she won't go deep.

The older woman sitting next to me says: "Stay the course." I start to weep because, I tell her, it gets tiring. People get tiring. It seems to me we are talking of healing work, social justice work. She just sits with me, resolute that I need to keep doing the work. Then I wake up.

Isabelle begins the dream searching for a bathroom and then sits down because she is exhausted. She gives away a pair of shoes, as if she can no longer take another step. Yet then she receives a visitor, a young woman who offers her encouragement: "Stay the path!" The racialized segregation of the first part of the dream then becomes a multicolored ecosystem of water creatures—the just, beautiful, and diverse world Isabelle seeks.

The first dream guide, who turns out to be a mermaid, takes Isabelle's daughter swimming with the dolphins, though Isabelle jokes she is not yet ready to "go deep." The daughter (who perhaps embodies a younger Isabelle, or perhaps the next generation of activists) is just beginning to encounter the Presence, to descend to the temple below.

Meanwhile, Isabelle sits on the shore with the older dream guide. The older messenger has almost exactly the same message as the younger one: "Stay the course." Isabelle is a woman of color working on intractable issues of oppression, and she is exhausted. The older woman listens, yet is resolute that Isabelle must continue to do her work. The loving witness this dream healer provides is a healing for Isabelle. While she may not always feel able to express her exhaustion and frustration in waking life, the dream makes space for those feelings.

The dream affirms Isabelle's efforts to bring justice to a world where oppression still thrives, and also acknowledges that this work is difficult. The dream healing here also comes in the form of water, and water creatures who bring delight, relaxation, and comfort. Surrounded by these companions, Isabelle can let her tears flow—connecting her personal waters with the vast waters of the ocean—and in this way, find new strength to go on changing the world. Isabelle is now part of a group that supports Jewish women of color. She continues to work toward decolonization, supported by others who are doing the same—just as in the dream.

PRACTICE WHAT YOU DREAM

Some healing dreams can offer us a new direction in life, showing us a path forward that we might not otherwise have found.

Peter is serving a long prison sentence after a life marked by addiction. Over the course of many months, Peter shared numerous dreams with me, and expressed his visions of how he might rebuild his life, his relationships, and his work in safe and healthy ways. Throughout that time, Peter also began having a series of dreams which offered him insight into how he might evolve his way of being in the world. The first dream was as follows:

> *My family and I live in a beautiful castle-like house on a plateau. There is a waterfall in our side yard. My father and I take care of animals; he drives around with his wagon, fixing and building enclosures for the animals. We have pet lions, dolphins, sea lions. There's a cat sanctuary with leopards, cheetahs, lynxes. My mother has a pet fox. All the animals are very friendly. I keep having different versions of this dream, as if the dream keeps evolving.*

Within this dream's friendly animals, safe in their enclosures, Peter can see his own need for safe boundaries, so both he and the people around him can be free from harm. That Peter's father builds the enclosures is touching: Peter's father is the person he loves and trusts most.

Reflecting on the dream, Peter says: "In a way, I'm like any animal . . . I don't want to bite anyone, but sometimes I can't control my crazy behavior." The dream suggests to Peter that his struggle is real, and that he can be part of society if he is able to "build enclosures" for his impulses.

I ask Peter what the healing message in the dream is. Peter says he thinks he should work with animals when he leaves prison. Later, he reports many other dreams of caring for animals, including one where he works at a marine center, swimming with and caring for hurt seals, walruses, dolphins, whales, and sharks. A white bird follows him, sleeping on his pillow and affectionately nipping his nose. The white bird perhaps shows Peter an image of himself as playful rather than harmful. These dream images are pointing Peter in the direction of caring for animals, and being cared for by animals in turn. Thus, he has the possibility of receiving unconditional love and a new start in life.

Peter comments:

I know whatever I choose to do, it will probably be with wildlife. I'd love to work with all the sea animals. They are, for the most part, very peaceful. There is lots of work I can do with animals all over the world.

Dreams so often know what medicine we need, if we are able to listen.

DREAM-HEALING
ACROSS MULTIPLE DREAMS

Sometimes our dream healing occurs not all in one dream, but over a series of related dreams. In such a case, receiving the healing requires noticing what is different as the dreams progress.

Tamara, a professor of comparative religion living in the Midwest, had twice before—during moments of transition in her intellectual life—dreamed that her mouth was fused shut. In those dreams, important men in her life helped her open her mouth and find her voice. But this third, related dream felt different.

> *I am outside in a forest. My mouth is fused shut, and I put my mouth on the bark of a tree to pry it open. It hurts a great deal and I cry out when it finally opens, but I am still happy about what has happened.*

This dream, and its predecessors, seemed to Tamara "an obvious metaphor for the way I feel frustrated by my inability to speak authentically as a scholar in my own voice." In the first two dreams, Tamara's respected colleagues helped her. Tamara explained: "This [third] dream wasn't responding to an externally-imposed transition, but rather came as I was trying to think through what kind of scholar I want to be. I have friends, sources of inspiration and people I love in my life, but there was something in this dream about needing . . . not exactly to do it on my own, but to get a different kind of help in a new way."

Tamara, who works to help Christians and Jews understand one another, notes that a "tree" in Jewish symbolism can refer to the Tree of Life, and it can also refer to the Cross in Christian tradition. This universal Tree, which transcends the boundaries of religions, is the healing Presence in the dream, and it is the source and support of Tamara's unique voice and vision of peace and understanding between religions and cultures. It is this Tree that comes to let her voice be heard.

When you wake from a dream, make a habit of noticing if there is healing in it.

Is there a wound in your dream? If so, what kind? It could be anything from a dream injury to paralysis to a sense of shame. For instance, Isabelle's wound was in the exhaustion she expressed. Tamara's wound was in her fused-shut mouth.

Now, see if you can tell who the healer is in your dream. How does the healer tend the dream wound? With words, touch, medicine?

What makes you feel good or helps you heal in the dream? Are you immersing in water, eating nourishing food, listening to music, lying on the earth, receiving healing touch? How might such dream moments suggest a healing for you in waking life?

If you're uncertain, you can use journaling or meditation to ask the healing characters, or even the wound itself, for more information about the area of your life that needs attention. Or you can bring the dream to a friend or a dream circle for further exploration.

If you have had a healing dream, it's important to apply the dream healing in the waking world if you can. If the dream invites you to rest, or take in some kind of healing medicine, consider whether it might be wise to do that. If there's a person the dream indicates you need to see, and it's safe and possible to do so, make a visit to that person or give them a call. If there's a change in your life the dream suggests, consider whether the dream might be right.

If you had a hot bath in the dream, try having one in the real world and see what happens. If there's a plant or a food in the dream that is a healing element, consider incorporating that element in your waking life. For example, I might advise Tamara to take a walk in a forest, since the dream invites her to connect to a tree.

In my dream about being offered a jar of witch hazel, the witch hazel turned out to bring real healing to a physical ailment of mine. Consider the possibility the dream is offering a literal medicine for your ailments in the real world.

Show reverence for the healers in the dream. If a plant, element, or animal helped you, build a relationship with that plant or animal. Make a sacred spot in your home to remember the dream. Or go out into the fields, onto the beach, etc., and connect to the being(s) that healed you.

If you have an ailment or a problem that needs healing, you can ask the dreamworld to send help. Before sleep, take a moment to ask for the healing you need. While not all of our ailments can be healed in dreams, the healing that dreams can and do provide is astounding.

CHAPTER 6

Ancestral Healing in Our Dreams

Death, in tribal cultures, initiates a metamorphosis wherein the person's presence does not "vanish" from the sensible world (where would it go?) but rather remains as an animating force within the vastness of the landscape, whether subtly, in the wind, or more visibly, in animal form. . . . The familiar human embodiment dies and decays to become part of the encompassing cosmos.

—David Abram[1]

In the 1930s, a young Jewish girl named Tola Pszenica contracted scarlet fever. One night her fever rose to such a degree that doctors did not believe she would survive. A *minyan* of her relatives stood at her bedside, praying.

That night, Tola dreamed that her great-grandmother and namesake, Tobe Sure, came to her with some beautiful ripe plums, saying: "Eat these nourishing plums, my dear, and you will soon be well again. Don't be afraid." Within the dream, the girl ravenously bit into the fruit. Her fever broke that night.

While the girl had never seen her great-grandmother, when she described the details of what the woman was wearing, her grandfather exclaimed that he knew exactly the garment Tola was describing. He searched his belongings for the brown jumper, and Tola confirmed it was exactly the article of clothing she had seen in the dream.[2]

A Sephardic Jewish mother in Edirne tells a similar tale, in which her father came to her in a dream to offer a cure for her sick child:

> One day he had a big [infected sore] on his head. He was a year old by then. I put him in a *kunika de aire* [a cradle covered with netting]. My father appeared in a dream. And the toilet was far from the house. I would put a large pot in the house, and all the children would urinate in it, because in the winter they couldn't go out. My father is telling me "Take the pot, put a rag inside, put it on his head, and he won't have anything else." And I took it without saying a word ... I got up in the morning, the child is sleeping, the child is not crying ... he was okay. When the doctor came, he confirmed that urine was the best thing [for that ailment].[3]

The ancestors often come to us in our dreams. Like other dream guides, they are messengers from the cosmos, citizens of the underground temple, elemental beings—part of everything, and still very much part of our lives. They bring us healing, comfort, wisdom, and love. People around the world report their beloved dead appearing to them in dreams, sometimes at the moment of death, and sometimes long afterward.

THE PEAR TREE:
MY DREAM JOURNEY WITH MY FATHER

My father, of blessed memory, died a few years ago. He was eighty-three and had lived a full life, though I wanted him to stay longer. He was a dentist, yet his true passions were woodworking, fixing broken things, and caring for his land. He was a beloved presence in my life, and we took great joy in one another. A few months before he died, I had a dream that let me know his time was short.

> *I am at my parents' house. I haven't brought them gifts and I feel badly. My mother shows me a tiny withered plant in a pot, maybe an orchid. The plant has lovely pale pink flowers and a magnificent smell. I am astonished by how fragrant it is.*
>
> *I go out on the deck with my father. Near the deck, there is an enormous, magnificent pear tree in bloom. My father keeps pointing at the tree and telling me to look. I say that I see the tree and it is lovely, but he tells me to go closer. When I walk across the deck to its edge, I see white pear flowers strewn all over the lawn.*

In my dream, I feel inadequate to properly gift my parents, yet they have gifts for me: they are showing me the story of their lives. During my visit, it becomes clear that the plants and the people are the same. My mother is the tiny, withered but fragrant orchid. She, it turns out, will remain alive for years to come even with her frail body.

My father is the pear tree with falling blossoms. (The tree in that spot in waking life is a sycamore, but my father did also tend pear trees.) I am awestruck by the beauty and majesty of the tree. Yet my father insists I walk close enough to see the carpet of pear blossoms on the grass. He wants me to see that the flowers are falling—his life is coming to an end. And he wants me to see that the flowers are beautiful even when they have fallen. Life is no less wondrous because it ends. My father is showing me the entire cycle, from seed to growth to death. That was his way in life, to love the earth and to accept the real.

A few months after the first dream, a week before my father's death, I dreamed another dream:

My father is having his second bar mitzvah. I am reciting the prayers. He gets up and gives a speech about how we should all love one another. I am full of joy to be with him at this event. Later, while I am in bed, I get a phone call from him, thanking me. He sounds happy.

Then, I get another telephone call. My dad tells me he needs help getting home. I ask where he is and he says he's in the park, calling from a store. He sounds weak. I tell him I will come right away and he should rest and wait for me. I throw on clothes and rush out the door to find my father. I think that he must have been enjoying the fresh air.

There is a little-known Jewish custom that when a person reaches the age of eighty-three (thirteen plus seventy) they may have a second coming of age, a second bar or bat mitzvah. My father never had such a ceremony—indeed, he spent very little time in synagogue at all—but he was eighty-three when he died. In my father's dream "bar mitzvah speech," he is telling me the sum total of his life's wisdom, which is that we must love one another. He is, in a sense, coming of age, completing his journey in this body. He is happy and he thanks me (a detail that still moves me).

In the second part of the dream, my father is frail and needs help "to get home."

It is clear the "home" is not his physical home but his soul's home: wherever he is going next. He asks me for help, and I immediately rush out to find him.

Yet when I had this dream, I didn't immediately realize what it meant: that my father was imminently dying. This is still heartbreaking for me. I saw my father two days before his death, and I assured him that I loved him, but I am not sure I helped him "get home" in the way he requested in the dream. It wasn't easy for my father to talk about dying, and I never wanted to distress him by bringing it up. Looking back on it, I wish I had made more space for him to try.

My dreams of my father offered me comfort and healing in my grief; they let me know my father had lived the purpose of his life and that he was grateful to me for loving him. Yet after my father's death, I struggled a great deal with the end of my second dream. I was close with my father and at peace with him, but it was painful for me that I hadn't been there when he died, that I hadn't understood the message of the dream.

It was also not comforting that my father's dream of his own death, which he shared with me a few weeks before he died, was a troubling one. In his dream, soldiers were planning to plant a bomb in his body, even as he protested. My father knew, in spite of the obscuring medical language all around him, that his living body was approaching its end. That dream reflected his experience of Western medicine, in which his body was treated as a broken machine rather than as a dying person.

Yet my father also had another, kinder vision of his death. A few weeks before he died, as he waited for surgery, sedated and half asleep, my father began to tell me what he was seeing. "I saw a woman dressed in green, eating a salad," he told me. "The salad had olives in it, and the olives were jumping up and down. One of the olives got away, and you tried to catch it, but I said: 'Let it go, Jill!'"

In this dream, my father is receiving healing as death approaches. He perceives a woman in green—we might call her a Green Woman, a human embodiment of the green and vibrant earth. One of her "olives" gets away. The word "olive," as my wife later pointed out, sounds like "I'll live." The olive, of course, is my father.

When I try to stop the olive from vanishing out of the salad, my father tells me to "let it go." When I feel back into that moment, I think my father is saying: "Let me go." His dream is a message that life comes and goes, and we must both accept this as part of our human condition. This waking dream held the healing that he needed, and that I needed, to move forward.

When I think of my father's vision, I am comforted. I know he would not want me to dwell on his last days, or on what I did not do. He would want me to think of his bar mitzvah party and of how he told me about the importance of love. He is in the care of the Green Woman now, and what he wants me to remember is how much we loved each other. For me, my father is and will always be the pear tree—the luxuriant, blossoming body of a life fully lived.

I PROMISE IT WILL BE OKAY:
ANCESTRAL VISITATIONS

When I asked friends and colleagues for their experiences of ancestor dreams, Joanna, a psychiatrist, shared a healing dream of her father with me: "While my father was readying himself and us for his death, my older son, who has autism and psychiatric illnesses, was quietly getting extremely ill. After my father died, my son G. had to be hospitalized for two months and receive electroconvulsive therapy. So I couldn't mourn properly. About one year after my father's death, my son was far from well and talking about suicide."

One night, my father came to me in a dream. It felt like a great surprise—like I came around a corner, preoccupied, and there he was, as real as life. I called out, "Daddy, Daddy!" My dad smiled at me, and said, "Here I am."

He opened his arms and I walked into his embrace. He whispered to me, "I just want you to know I am very much okay. It's very peaceful. I'm looking after D. [Joanna's sister, who died of suicide years ago] now and things are getting brighter and brighter. Don't worry, G. is going to be okay. I know it looks pretty bleak now, but I promise it will be okay."

I woke up then, stunned, disoriented, profoundly comforted. I knew even in that semi-daze that this was not an ordinary dream, that I had indeed been visited by my father.

Joanna's experience of being "visited" is an experience shared by many who dream of deceased loved ones. In these visitation dreams, the loved one's tangible presence brings comfort to the living dreamer. In Joanna's dream, her father offers a prophecy—his ill grandson will be healed—and a promise that the dreamer's deceased sister is no longer suffering.

This dream held healing for Joanna, opening channels between herself and her sister and giving her hope for her son. Joanna felt a new connection with her sister's spirit as a result of her father's promise. This dream healed Joanna of her stuck grief and allowed her to bravely face the challenges in her life.

Dreams of our beloved dead or ancestral presences bring us wisdom that goes beyond anything we consciously know. Such dreams embody a love that is passed down through generations. These dreams acknowledge grief, but also allow us to transcend it. They offer us entry into a healing Place where life and death can meet.

PASSING DOWN ANCESTRAL GIFTS

Sometimes, ancestor dreams contain not only an encounter, but a transmission of gifts from one generation to the next. Here, Sasha, the healer we met in Chapter One, describes a powerful dream she experienced the night before her grandmother died:

> *The very old pine tree in front of my childhood home has been struck by lightning. It falls down and creates a maze and shelter on the front lawn that I am running through. I am being chased through the branches by a gigantic owl. I am trying to find a place to hide, but the owl seizes me by the nape of my neck and throws me down. We wrestle for what seems like hours. I am out of breath.*

The owl pins me to the ground with its great wing arms and stares at me with very human eyes. It says, "Surrender, and this will be much easier." Then it bites my arm with its great beak. I cry out and then quiet my body. Something warm and intense flows into my body through my bloodstream and I pass out. After a while, the owl touches my arm with their feathers and the cut closes up and heals completely, though there is still a scar and my arm aches and stings. The owl looks up into the sky and says, "It is done. The gifts are in you now," and flies off.

The next morning, my mother calls me and tells me my grandmother died in the night.

Sasha's grandmother loved owls, working as a rehabilitator at a raptor refuge through her eighties. The owl also has mythic resonance: it is associated with the wild demoness Lilith, the Greek goddess Athena, the Welsh goddess Blodeuwedd, and other spirit entities. The owl is an embodiment of wise, often feminine, Presence.

As Sasha's grandmother leaves the world, she chooses Sasha as one who will carry on her legacy—and indeed, around the time of the dream, Sasha had begun training with an intuitive healer. The dream was an initiation into her gifts. Today, Sasha pursues a healer's path, as did many of her female ancestors (including her grandmother, who was a healer of birds).

The wrestling in this dream also connects Sasha to her biblical ancestors. In Genesis 32, Jacob wrestles all night with a mysterious entity before receiving both a wound on his thigh and a new name: Israel (meaning "God-wrestler"). Similarly, Sasha wrestles with the owl and receives a transformative wound. Although she does not explicitly receive a new name, the gift from her grandmother enters her bloodstream and changes her.

HEALING THE PAST AND THE FUTURE

Jewish tradition offers many visions of what happens after death. Stories in the Talmud and other Jewish sources speak of souls delighting in the Garden of Eden, or being gathered with other souls in a kind of treasury beneath God's throne. Still other Jewish traditions, such as the twelfth-century kabbalistic work Sefer haBahir and Hayyim Vital's sixteenth-century work Sha'ar haGilgulim (the Gate of Reincarnations), suggest that souls may return in new bodies. There are many Jewish traditions—such as the Eastern European tradition of making soul candles to commemorate the dead and ask them for their help in the affairs of the living, or the tradition of inviting one's dead parents to a wedding[4]—that invoke the ongoing Presence of our ancestors in our lives. There is a Jewish sense not only that another life beyond this one exists, but that the ancestors are still in contact and community with us.

We have many Jewish records of dreams of the ancestors in which they give warning or demonstrate their connection to us. The seventeenth-century Jewish woman diarist Glückel of Hameln, for example, tells of a relative's dream in which his recently deceased wife came to him to complain that her shroud was missing; when he had her grave dug up, he found that this was in fact true, and the women of the community set about making a new shroud. In another story, Glückel reports that, at the moment of an elderly relative's death, a child of the family dreamed there was an old bearded man in his bed. These dreams were taken seriously as genuine visitations from ancestral spirits.[5]

Lior is a rabbi who lives in Massachusetts. When Lior's grandfather was starving in a concentration camp, he dreamed his deceased mother would feed him huge warm meals she had made. These dream meals sustained him. Guided by this legacy, Lior strongly believes in the power of ancestral dreams.

While discussing their dreams, Lior recalled that their grandmother—who had survived the Holocaust—would pray to God throughout the day in Yiddish, and that she considered God to be her closest friend. Lior then shared with me a dream of their grandmother in which they discovered her powerful, secret legacy.

> About three weeks after my grandmother died, I dreamed that I found a secret necklace that belonged to her. It was covered with Hebrew letters and new prayers I had never seen. The centerpiece was a huge maroon bead that had writing carved in it, all about the Shekhinah! I had the sense that the larger beaded part of the necklace represented Hashem [the masculine aspect of deity], while the maroon centerpiece represented the Shekhinah [the feminine aspect of deity].
>
> The necklace felt otherworldly: I was holding it in my hands, but it wasn't completely of the physical realm. I was so overcome with emotion that my grandmother had this secret relationship with the Shekhinah that I hadn't known about. I wanted to learn more about this relationship.

Devotion to the feminine aspect of the Divine is here depicted as a precious secret, and one that can be recovered. Lior notes that they "felt sad, in awe, and also very surprised" upon making this dream discovery. These feelings echo those of many in our generation who are discovering long-marginalized Jewish traditions about the feminine aspects of God.

Lior also noted the dream necklace had the feel of being from the otherworld. This suggests the necklace was an ancestral gift, connecting Lior with their deceased grandmother. Lior adds that there was a "sweet residue when I awoke from this dream, like I had been between worlds."

In the dream, Lior discovered a grandmother's secret and also a hidden face of the Jewish tradition: teachings of the kabbalists in which God is masculine and feminine, transcendent and immanent. The joining of these aspects of God is considered a *tikkun*, a healing of the cosmos. And the reclamation of the feminine, after centuries of marginalization and denigration, is also a profound healing that points us toward a more inclusive future.

This ancestral dream points Lior toward this *tikkun* in their own life, and toward a connection with Shekhinah, the immanent face of the Divine. Indeed, inspired by their grandmother, Lior is currently writing a thesis on Yiddish women's prayers. If I were to give Lior further dream advice, I would suggest they consider making a necklace as an embodiment of the dream. Embodying one's dream in the physical world can have real power and uncover new thoughts and feelings; such a charged material item could also become a powerful focus for prayer or meditation.

LIVE THE LIFE WE COULD NOT LIVE:
HEALING ANCESTRAL TRAUMA

Not all ancestral dreams are pleasant. A whole genre of dreams deals with our ancestors' trauma and its impact on us. Rabbi Tirzah Firestone recalls a dream of her relatives who perished in the Holocaust.

> *In my twenty-fifth year, I dreamed of a slender Hungarian woman dressed in a fur coat. Beneath her lavish attire, I saw that she was, in fact, a naked skeleton, peering at me with both*

irony and affection. The woman could see that I was young and raw, paralyzed by an unnamed guilt, barely able to buy myself a teapot or a secondhand sweater without being assailed by self-doubt.

Dahlink, she called to me, her thick accent comforting and somehow familiar: Don't be a fool! Don't you think we would be enjoying our beautiful things if we could? *Her jaw clacked with boney laughter.*

Suddenly the lights went on and the room filled with richly clad Hungarian ladies, skeletons all, enjoying a tea party. It was clear that they were all dead, yet they were also radiant and full of life. Turning toward me, their voices rose in unison: Do you think it helps us that you suffer? Live the life we could not live!

I sat up in bed and wept. Their words had penetrated me, touching the core of my malaise, an outsized case of survivor's guilt I did not know I had. Live the life we could not live! *These words became a turning point, a mantra, a north star. I took them with me as I found my footing in the world.*[6]

Astonishingly, Firestone did not actually know that her Hungarian relatives had met their deaths in concentration camps—not until looking into her family history after she had this dream. The dream revealed to her the cause of her poorly understood guilt and anxiety. Firestone writes: "The silence shrouding a family's untold stories paradoxically becomes the strongest form of transmission . . . Many of us struggle to bring to consciousness the hidden legacies that our families bequeath to us."[7]

The profoundly disturbing images in the dream—skeletons in fur coats and rich clothes—embody the paradox of Hungarian Jews who were life-affirming and prosperous yet died dishonored and disrobed at the hands of the Nazis. The dream directly addresses the survivor's guilt, unease, and malaise that children and grandchildren of survivors often feel. The message of the skeletons at their tea party is simple: "Enjoy life. That's all we wanted to do."

Firestone deeply received the healing of this dream. She took charge of her life, became a psychotherapist, was ordained as a rabbi, and rediscovered her deep soul-connection to Judaism. Today, she offers workshops on ancestral healing, aiding others in taking the healing journey she took.

Ancestral trauma dreams give us the possibility of processing and releasing trauma we have stored in our bodies and memories. These dreams also give us the option of more authentic relationships with our ancestors. Working through this material can be a profound gift, allowing us to be more present in our bodies and lives.

DREAM-TENDING THE ANCESTORS

Sometimes we meet not a specific ancestor, but the ancestors as a plural entity—the mythic ancestors, the chain of generations. Esther, a kohenet from the Midwest, dreamed of tending the ancestors: letting them know they are honored, remembered, and loved.

> *In my dream, I see an altar. On the altar are a lot of candles burning. There is a woman there in a full gown. She is teaching me about the altar. She is pleasant and loving.*

> *I notice that the air is very good. Even though the candles are smoking, I can still breathe. The air is the best air you ever wanted to breathe. I say: "Where am I?" I look up expecting to see the sky. Instead, I see the bottoms of caskets suspended high above me. It is as if the caskets are buried in the ground and I am even deeper underground. Then I get startled and wake up.*

In this dream, Esther is standing at an altar covered with candles. A kind and caring woman in a formal gown teaches her how to tend the altar. We might say this woman is a *maggid*, a spirit guide—or the Presence Herself.

When I ask what the altar-keeper's message is, Esther is clear: "She is teaching me what my altar is supposed to look like . . . I believe that the candles we burn at our altars can extend their energy to the underground world so healing can take place." After this fire-tending dream, Esther took the dream's advice and began to use candles in rituals to honor her ancestors.

This candle-lighting practice has deep roots in Jewish tradition. Jews light candles to honor the soul of a person who has passed, during the mourning period and on the *yahrtzeit*, the yearly anniversary of their death. In Jerusalem, elderly Jewish women regularly light candles at family tombs to ask for the intercession of ancestors in the lives of their descendants,[8] and all over the world, Jews light candles at the tombs of saints and righteous people.

Indeed, Esther's dream has resonance with earlier dreams of ancestral encounters. In 1608, in the city of Tzfat, a colleague of the kabbalist Hayyim Vital named Rabbi Elijah Amiel had a dream in which he and Hayyim Vital gathered many Jewish ancestors and went on a pilgrimage to the Temple in Jerusalem. The pair gathered more and earlier ancestors, including kabbalist

Moses Cordovero, *halakhah* scholar Joseph Caro, Rabbi Akiva, Yochanan ben Zakkai, and other great lights of the Talmud. Finally, Vital writes, they encountered the earliest biblical ancestors:

> *Adam, Abraham, Isaac, and Jacob—these four were not buried in the earth, but were sleeping in a cave and there was a very large torch before Adam. Innumerable lights and flames were incorporated in the large flame of the torch, from top to bottom. Rabbi Elijah asked me: What are these flames? [I told him:] These are the souls of all the righteous which are incorporated in the soul of Adam.*[9]

The candles burning on Esther's altar to honor the ancestors seem related to this four-hundred-year-old dream in which the flames in the underground temple of Adam's tomb are the souls of all who have lived since the time of creation.

In myths and cultures the world over, the soul is often envisioned as a flame. Thus, lighting fires to honor and tend the ancestors is a custom in many traditions around the world. Just to give a few examples: Catholics, too, light candles to bring blessing to the dead; the Herero people of southern Africa light the *okuruuo* fire to indicate the contact between the living and the dead;[10] and at Chinese funerals and ancestor-honoring rituals, gifts are cast into a fire in order that the gifts be transmitted to the ancestors.[11]

We might say Esther's dream is meant to transform her waking spiritual life, because it invites her into a practice of ancestor-tending using flame. Yet it is also a dream in which the ancestors ask Esther to tend and heal them. This ongoing honoring of relationships is another way we attend to the ancestors as emissaries of the Presence.

If you've had a dream of someone who has died, the first thing I recommend is offering gratitude, and then writing down the details of the dream (as always): these details may be important to your relationship with that person or group of people. If the dream feels like a communication, take that seriously. These dreams often provide crucial healing, advice, and witness for the living.

If the message is clear, consider how you want to address the message in waking life. If the message isn't clear, go back to the dream image in your mind and ask the ancestor what the message is. See if you hear a reply.

You may also feel called to tend that ancestor: by lighting a candle, finding a picture of them, or eating a food they loved. Having a place in the house dedicated to ancestors (with photographs, letters, or things they owned) can be a helpful way to acknowledge their presence in your life. There are many Jewish ways to tend ancestors, from the *kaddish* (memorial prayer) to *yizkor* (special prayers of remembrance on holidays) to lighting a *yahrt-zeit* (year-anniversary) candle. Pilgrimages to graves, particularly before the new year, are also traditional.

If your dream is frightening or difficult, see what issue is being identified as the problem and how you can address that issue. You can set up an empty chair and speak to your ancestor, imagining them in the empty chair, if there's something you need to get off your chest or apologize for. Empty chairs are a long-standing Jewish way to represent ancestral presences: consider the chair of Elijah at a circumcision, the chair placed for ancestor-spirits in some Sephardic *sukkot*, or the chair of Miriam that nineteenth-century pregnant women in Jerusalem set up for protection during difficult labors.[12]

If your ancestor dream feels like it is tapping into negative aspects of your relationship with that person in ways that don't feel productive, it's okay to "clear" the dream and let it go. Take a bath or a shower, or go out and sit on the earth. Also, you can set a boundary if the visitation is unwelcome, asking that ancestor not to visit, or not until you're ready.

An ancestor dream often provokes great emotion, whether joy or sorrow. Tending oneself carefully after such a dream is wise. Decide carefully whether to share such dreams with family or friends—whether you will get the support you need, or a more difficult reaction.

Finally, you can invite ancestor dreams before you go to sleep, welcoming loving presences to visit you if they wish. I invite my ancestors who come in dreams to keep coming: to comfort me, relieve my sadness, strengthen my gifts, and make me less afraid of my own finite being. You can use a prayer like this one, based on a Yiddish women's prayer for making soul candles:

> *Azoy vi mir hobn nisht fargesn in di heylike neshomes, zoln mir oykh geda-kht vern tsum gutn. Ven ikh leyg zikh avek shlofn, zoln balibte neshomes mir bazukhn, araynfirndik tikn un heylung. Zoln libevdike ureltern mikh bentshn mit zeyer onveznhayt. Omeyn.*

> As we have not forgotten the holy souls, so may we be remembered for good. As I lie down to sleep, may beloved souls visit me for transformation and for healing. May loving ancestors grace me with their presence. Amen.[13]

CHAPTER 7

Dream·Healing Our World

The earth never runs out of messages. But humans as a species have lost touch with this reality. The majority of the human population lives in urban areas where we consume and live processed lives. It is no wonder too few of us make grand changes in our lives concerning excessive consumerism and waste. How can we think of what we do not encounter?

—LaChelle Schilling[1]

Today we are faced with a challenge that calls for a shift in our thinking, so that humanity stops threatening its life-support system. We are called to assist the Earth to heal her wounds and in the process heal our own—indeed, to embrace the whole creation in all its diversity, beauty and wonder.

—Wangari Maathai[2]

Personal and ancestral healing within the dream temple are both critical parts of our journey. However, as I collected more and more dreams for this book, it became clear that some dreams are not about individual journeys, but about our collective journey as a species and an ecosystem. At some point, we must consider the needs of the temple itself.

Our world-temple, our planet that holds us within its web of ecologies, is threatened. We know it in our waking lives, and we also perceive it on a deep level beneath our conscious minds. We are, after all, made of the elements and minerals, of the plant and animal worlds. Our bodies are quite literally part of the earth. And as conscious beings, we perceive our world changing—we experience in our bodies that the climate is altered and that ecosystems around us are imperiled or already lost, whether or not we are thinking about those sobering truths in daily life. So it makes sense that we dream of planetary crisis and human alienation. Blessedly, we also dream of how to heal our world.

Dreaming of our relationship to and impact upon the natural world has an ancient history. In Genesis 41, the Pharaoh of Egypt dreams two dreams. In the first dream, seven healthy cows come out of the Nile, and then seven emaciated cows come out of the Nile and swallow the seven healthy cows. In the second dream, Pharaoh sees a grain stalk with seven healthy ears sprout out of the ground, but then a withered grain stalk sprouts and devours the stalk with seven healthy ears. Pharaoh asks many dream interpreters but none can offer a satisfactory interpretation of the dream. Only Joseph, a Hebrew slave who has been languishing in prison, is able to tell him that the two dreams are really one dream, and that Pharaoh has dreamt of the future of his people and land. There will be seven years of abundance followed by seven years of famine. Egypt must prepare, Joseph says, if they are to be spared. Pharaoh immediately understands that the dream is a true dream and Egypt must prepare for what is to come.

Like Pharaoh, we are dreaming true dreams of danger to our lands. At the time of this writing, California, Australia, Siberia, and the Amazon are on fire, and the polar ice is melting at an alarming rate. However, as Sally Gillespie, a depth psychologist and the author of *Living the Dream: A Guide to Working with Your Dreams*, writes: "As the old world is destroyed, opportunities arise to heal ancient divisions and to find renewal."[3] The earth is calling to us in our dreams, imploring us to awaken while there is still time. The good news is that our dreams, like Pharaoh's, can offer remedies and healing for our collective life on the earth.

The Zohar explains that Shekhinah, the Presence dwelling in the world, is the *nefesh*, the soul of the animate universe, and "She makes of all things a single, whole body."[4] In this sense, we do not merely experience the Presence; we *are* the Presence, and we feel the pull of the larger whole. Right now, this life force, the soul of the world-organism, is dreaming within us what our ecosystem needs to come back into balance.

Many kabbalistic sources express a sense of the physical world's alienation from the sacred. The Shekhinah, the Presence, has been separated from Her proper state of union with the transcendent worlds—this is called Her exile. In his book *The Gates of Holiness,* the kabbalist Hayyim Vital states that all our righteous acts are meant "to liberate the Shekhinah from exile."[5] The kabbalah at its core asserts that repair is possible, that the Presence and the world can return to wholeness. In our current planetary situation, we have to hope and believe that the mystics' intuition is correct.

THE SALMON RETURN:
COMING BACK TO EARTH

All through this book, we have been considering how dreams call us to an awareness of the larger cosmos. This is especially important in an age when society tends to disconnect us from nature. Consider this dream, shared with me by an artist and kohenet I'll call Ivy:

> *I've gone back to my home state of Minnesota. Without saying anything to my family, I leave the house and go for a walk. I come to a body of water where people have gathered to marvel at the salmon. It's a miracle that the salmon have returned. I say a prayer that the salmon may continue to return in abundance. I see across the way some abandoned, flooded houses where poor folks live.*
>
> *I get in the water, which appears to me to be shallow. I want to go down to the bottom and bounce back up. I go down deeper and deeper, yet not reaching the bottom. Finally I meet the earth, and then I'm stuck, and not able to rise. I realize I'm wearing a backpack that must be heavy from a computer and I take it off. I also somehow take in air. I wake up as the combination of the air and the lightened load allows me to rise from the depths.*

Ivy's dream takes place in the context of a natural world out of balance. The salmon's return is a welcome surprise in an age of extinction. The abandoned, flooded houses at the beginning of the dream suggest environmental devastation. Ivy is dreaming the truth that our environment is threatened. But the salmon always knows its way home, and the dreamer, too, has found the way to the watery womb of origin.

Drawn by the water, Ivy plunges in and heads for the bottom. They have a desire to touch mud, to swim down and back. But when Ivy gets to the earth at last, deep under the water's surface, Ivy becomes stuck and unable to move. What is wrong? Ivy discovers a heavy computer in their backpack. A computer, of course, is the very item that keeps most of us from connecting to our surroundings. The virtual world, as useful and compelling as it is, draws us away from full presence. The heavy computer is a manifestation of alienation from the body, the natural world, and our identity as an integrated part of all things. What's weighing Ivy down is weighing all of us down.

But when Ivy is free from the backpack, Ivy is able to breathe underwater—at home among the elements, like the salmon. Ivy takes in a lungful of air, rises back toward the surface, and awakens. Like the salmon, Ivy has returned home to the world that sustains and embraces them.

Ivy's immersion in the lake is a dream-healing moment, and it is also a return to Ivy's own true nature as a citizen of planet Earth. Our felt separation from nature is at the root of our existential exile. This dream asks that the dreamer put down the computer, encounter the physical world in all its tangibility and beauty, and come back into balance with the larger world-organism of which they are an integral part.

DREAMING THE PROBLEM

Dreams can diagnose the need for connection to nature, not just in individuals, but in the wider world. Such dreams force us to pay attention to what is happening around us. Jemma is a dream-worker, and her dream practice is dedicated to breaking cycles of trauma and suffering. Jemma shared this dream with me when I told her I was seeking dreams about global warming:

> *I am at my summer camp in Mississippi. We are running through the woods, and I realize that a pack of polar bears and wolves is*

> *chasing us. We hide behind a tree, then gather*
> *in a central field to protect ourselves.*
>
> *I cower with the camp director. He tells*
> *me that the polar bears are angry because it*
> *is too hot. He says they have come all the way*
> *down to Mississippi to warn us because of how*
> *hot they are. I turn and there is a polar bear on*
> *its hind legs, arms up. I am terrified. I receive a*
> *message from the polar bear: it is also terrified.*

The bear has come not to frighten Jemma, but to communicate its own terror. James Hillman teaches that dream animals are not symbols. They "are not images *of* animals, but images *as* animals."[6] In this dream, the bear is a real bear, and the bear has a right to be angry. The bear's presence says: "Look at me! See your impact on me and my species, and on the world we share." Through this dream, Jemma and the Great Bear discover one another's vulnerability. They are not enemies; they are part of the same planetary ecosystem. Now they must become allies. Our entwinement with all of life demands that we cast our lot with the other beings on our planet.

DREAMS CALL US TO ACTION

Dreams of ecological disaster sometimes call us to particular kinds of healing work. Francisco, a Native American man of Huichol and Spanish ancestry, is deeply engaged in traditional healing ceremonies. He first experienced this recurring dream when he was fifteen. Francisco explains: "In tenth grade, I had a lucid dream. It was the first time I dreamt in color."

> *My vision is split in half. My right eye pans to*
> *the right and sees a picnic scene. People are*

> *eating. A father is playing catch with his sons.*
> *There are families, adults, elders. There are*
> *trees, and there is blue sky. But in my left eye, I*
> *see charred earth and smoke. People are in dif-*
> *ferent stages of being burned. The dream shifts*
> *so I can see these scenes close up: a woman*
> *burned in the face, a child dying.*

Francisco told me: "When I woke up, I was out of breath as if I had been running. I didn't tell anyone about the dream. A month and a half later I had it again. This time the dream took place in a different country. The people looked European, but the pattern was the same: they were all being burnt."

"My father's sister is a medicine woman. I went and told her what happened. She said: 'You are seeing into the future. You will see this sometime in your life. You are being shown this for a reason.' She asked: 'Do you want help?' I said: 'I don't want this dream anymore.' She replied: 'Let's get together after the new moon.'"

Francisco's dream returned, but this time he willed himself to wake up. After the new moon, he went to see his aunt. She laid him down on the bed, lit a candle, and swept his body with a branch. Francisco recalls: "I felt air come in—the wind was lifting the sheet up and down as she was praying. I fell asleep during the prayer, and when I woke up, I felt something taken off me."

After the ceremony, the dream of fiery destruction never occurred again, but Francisco did begin to dream of himself praying over friends and family members. At first he ignored these dreams, but as time went on, he began to sit in ceremony and to learn healing practice. Over time, he became a healer like his aunt and other elders of his family. He turned the fear he experienced in the dream into a motivation to help others.

The split vision Francisco saw is the perfect image of the denial within which many of us live: we go on picnicking as the world burns. He says: "We are headed toward a dangerous precipice where there will be a catastrophe with lots of suffering. We can soften the impact by getting people to shift to a mindset of peace and resolution of conflict, internal and external. That dream, and what's coming, shapes why I do the work that I do. My people, the Huichol people, came to this world to teach about the sacredness of nature, the power of prayer, the power of communion with nature. We are teachers, medicine people; we are about creating new pathways." Francisco understands his dream as a call to healing and awareness on an individual and global level.

HEALING THE TEMPLE: VISIONS OF A HOPEFUL FUTURE

Some of the dreams we've seen in this chapter are terrifying. But people also dream of planetary renewal and of our capacity to change. Roxane, a parenting educator and community organizer in New York City, dreamed a dream in which humanity adapts to its situation. In her dream, the flooding of a city leads to a new human society.

> *I am on the rooftop of a house by the water and I am waiting for a tsunami. The water rises and then the houses are underwater. Everything is washed away by the flood. Then, I see that this is the beginning of a new world. The people grow gills. There is diversity among these evolved humans: some people are more like fish and some people are more like people. The houses, sometimes submerged by the tide and sometimes out in the air, have become a beautiful underwater city.*

Scientists debate whether to focus on mitigation of global warming, or on adaptation to what will be a radically different planet. Both approaches, of course, are needed. Roxane's dream focuses on adaptation, inviting us to imagine that, amid climate chaos, humans can survive and find a new and vibrant balance with their environment.

According to Grandmother Flordemayo, a Nicaraguan *curandera* (healer) and a member of the International Council of Thirteen Indigenous Grandmothers: "Our dreams are asking us to be ready for the changes that human presence on earth has caused, and help one another through them."[7] The Presence that spoke in Pharaoh's dreams is now speaking in ours. The question is, what will we do with these urgent messages?

When we are in touch with the web of life around us, we tap into the possibility of hope and renewal. Life holds astonishing creativity and regenerative power. If we align with the forces of life rather than denying them, new possibilities open: for instance, we can manage forests as carbon sinks, breed resilient coral reefs, or use mycelial networks to improve water quality.[8] Like the kabbalists who believed their every action could bring a little healing to the Divine Presence, we too can transform the world around us. Dreams can lead us where the life is.

WHEN DREAMS SHOW US OUR PATH

Often, when we have a dream, we may see it as a representation of something happening in our psyche. But what if we had the courage to make the dream a reality in the waking world?

While she was living on the West Coast, Skye's dreams repeatedly whispered sacred chants to her and showed her a volcanic island rising out of the sea. She knew these dreams were calling her to Hawaii, where she eventually traveled to learn traditional sacred practice and agriculture. (Skye, a woman of color, deeply identifies with Indigenous traditions.) "When I flew over the island," she remembers, "I felt I was entering my dream. I dropped to the ground and started to cry, saying: 'This is home.'"

In another of Skye's recurring dreams, she flew over the ocean and saw a volcanic island where people lived tribally.

> *I land in the forest. I find a basket for water and put it on my head. Two women come to accompany me, also with baskets. We walk up a mountain path. There are three pillars fixed in the ground, made of lava rock. On the pillars sits a sacred bowl. We sing the chant that I received in an earlier dream. A cloud forms and rains into the bowl.*

This sacred dream-ritual tells of the reverence of the Indigenous peoples for the water, the earth, and the cycles of life. This dream inspired Skye's eventual connection to Lake Waiau, a glacial lake high in the mountains, the foundation of the Hawaiian watershed. Lake Waiau is the only alpine glacial lake in the world, and is considered a sacred portal by the Hawaiian people. The lake is now under threat from a buildup of technology on its shores (particularly an overabundance of telescopes). Skye says: "I have been working on how to protect these peaks, and pray and work for waters around the world. We must protect these mountains and waters. We would not be able to live without our waters."

Skye is an example of a person who allowed a dream to direct the course of her life and show her how to contribute to the world's healing. Many of us, in large or small ways, are called by our dreams to make a contribution. We just have to pay attention.

When you begin to tune in to your ecological dreams, it may be hard to face what the dreams are saying. It is frightening to contemplate ecological catastrophe, and sobering to think of what our responsibility may be in this time. But the dreams can help us transform, if we let them.

Skye's dream drew her to take specific action to protect the sacred mountain and waters she witnessed in her dream. So too, you might have a dream that calls you to a specific role in the healing of the earth: to act on behalf of a specific place, being, or community. If you sense such a message in your dream, take it seriously. As the Talmud says, "You are not obligated to finish the work, but neither are you free to desist from it."[9] We each have a part to play in global healing.

See what happens when you don't read the images in the dream as symbols. If we dream of a flood, we might choose to read it as a symbol—of being "flooded" by feelings, for example. That can be an authentic reading of the dream. But we can also choose to see the flood as actual water—as a natural event we may be called to address. Then, the dream may call us to a different kind of response.

Ask yourself: How can I live the wisdom that has come to me in this dream? You can ask a character or landscape in the dream (like the bear in Jemma's dream): "What do you want of me? What is your message?" Listen within yourself for the answers to these questions. Identify allies in the dream (such as Ivy's salmon or Skye's water-bearers) who can support you and inspire you as you bring the dream's message into your waking life. Also, think about ways you might share the message of your dream with others.

Many people are suffering stress from ecological grief. People who are sensitive to the disaster that is unfolding in our world naturally feel overwhelmed by environmental crisis. Our dreams help us know we are not alone. We are in this together, part of the great whole. If there is comfort and hope in your dream, take that seriously too. The earth is often sending us messages that show us how to heal.

Within this collective context, what if we were to read our dreams of the ecosphere as a form of Torah? One year, my synagogue asked me to lead a Torah service. The Torah story for that Sabbath told of Pharaoh's dreams of famine, with which we began this chapter. I decided to gather the many global warming dreams I had collected, and the community recited them as part of the Torah reading, understanding those dreams as Torah for our time. There were many wet eyes in the congregation—and much desire to be part of transforming and repairing our world.

CHAPTER 8

Facing Our Nightmares

You've got to pray hard. Sometimes it will take months, years, even twenty years, and all of a sudden you will understand the dream.

—John (Bear) Tate[1]

If dreams are meant to take us to the Place that is Presence, then why are so many of them so scary? A mentor of mine, Dr. Catherine Shainberg, teaches that nightmares are meant to call attention to a pressing situation. They are particularly urgent diagnoses of the obstacles the dreamer faces within and without. Nightmares are unpleasant experiences, but they can be our friends. They can show us, with vivid clarity, what it is we are facing. The demons we encounter in nightmares, by embodying what we fear, ultimately work to our benefit, leading us deeper into our truths.

One of my scariest nightmares was a dream I remember from when I was eight or nine:

> *I am running along the road near the train tracks a quarter mile from my house. The tracks are on fire. Flames are shooting up from the ties, burning the trees all around. As I run, I feel that Satan is in my neighborhood, coming after my family. I know that I have to protect my parents and brother from him. There is a palpable miasma of evil; my skin crawls. I am running home as fast as I can, hoping I can get there before the flames do.*

Satan isn't a part of the religious tradition I grew up with as a child. To be honest, I'm not even sure how I knew about Satan. I probably saw a character on TV. Yet the dream was so terrifying I couldn't think about anything else, especially at night. Surrounded by stuffed animals, I camped outside my parents' bedroom door that night and for many nights afterward. I knew how angry my parents would be if I actually woke them, so I just kept watch in the hallway. I didn't dare tell anyone about the dream, but it haunted me for years.

What I didn't know then, but learned many years later, was that around this same time, my brother was having a recurring dream in which he lay paralyzed while a terrifying sound came closer and closer, getting louder and louder, shaking the earth all around. He had this dream many, many times over the course of his childhood. I think he and I were dreaming the same dream.

I trust my gut-level feeling that what I encountered in that dream was not just frightening, but real. At the time that I had this dream, my family was facing mental health crises that would consume us for decades. Looking back, I am certain the presence I perceived as demonic was an embodiment of the dysfunction afflicting my family. The Real was speaking to me as I slept, showing me what I already knew but couldn't fully integrate. Seeing this horror so clearly in the dream may have helped me face it in waking life.

The Talmud says: "If the eye were allowed to see them, no creature could withstand the demons; they are more numerous than we."[2] The Talmud also says that demons "have wings like ministering angels, and fly from one end of the world to the other like ministering angels, and know what will be in the future like the ministering angels."[3] In other words, the demons, too, are messengers. And the Zohar tells us that they come to us in dreams: "When a person is asleep in bed, the soul leaves and roams the world ... Numerous bands of dazzling demons traverse the world, and they accost that soul."[4]

According to the Talmud, the demons know what they know because they "listen behind the curtain" of the heavenly Temple.[5] We might understand from this that demons, too, open a portal to the Place. The demons in our dreams are goads and informants. They reveal scary things about our wounds, losses, fears, dangers, and resentments—about what is wrong in our lives and our world. Nightmares can alert us to harm, let us know what we are feeling, or spur us to change. They too can lead us where we need to go, if we are willing to follow where they lead.

THE DEMON DOOR:
DREAMS THAT TELL US THE BAD NEWS
AND WHAT TO DO ABOUT IT

Bette Ehlert is a dreamworker who, in the 1990s, facilitated dream groups in a women's prison. She records the following dream from one incarcerated woman named Juliette.

> *I am in a room, sitting with my boyfriend. Maybe we're talking. The room is dark. The only thing I can see clearly is Richard. I feel sad and scared. Something is wrong. The room has doors. Richard leaves. I don't see what door he goes out. He just disappears. I walk around and can't find him. I feel abandoned and sad. Then the doors fly open. Except one door. It's a rubber door. Something is pushing it. I run to it and hold it closed. I can see fingers pushing through the rubber. The fingers have nails like a beast. There is no light, nothing but darkness. I don't see anything. I'm screaming to Richard: "Come back! I want to go with you! I need help!" I don't want to let the door go and go after him. I need to hold the door. I am scared to even move.*[6]

In Juliette's nightmare, a terrifying beast lurks behind a rubber door, clawing its way toward her. But her boyfriend Richard, who abandons her, is the real villain of the dream. Richard, it turns out, involved Juliette in a violent robbery: he assaulted a man who had picked up the two of them while they were hitchhiking, and told Juliette to go through his pockets and take his valuables. Richard then escaped and Juliette was arrested for the crime. In the dream, Richard also "escapes," leaving Juliette to deal with the monster on her own.

In reflecting on the dream, Juliette also noticed that the sad and scary room reminded her of the closet where she would hide to escape her abusive grandmother and uncle. She saw the fingernails as being like those of her mother, who would beat her and lock her in her room. And she could also see the beast as herself, as she victimized another person during the robbery.

Juliette's dream showed her a frightening truth that she had been unable to integrate: she wanted to keep the beast (her own inner beast, and her abusers) out of her life, yet felt paralyzed and unable to summon help. But the landscape of the dream does also show Juliette a room in which there are other doors than the demon door. She might perhaps stop trying to hide, or hold back the demon, and instead choose a different door, one that is open instead of closed and frightening. Indeed, Juliette's dream group encouraged her to go back into the dream and perhaps find a way to make the dream outcome better.

THE VAMPIRE GIRL: HEALING OUR NIGHTMARES

Reentering a dream and allowing a different ending can be a way to work through trauma and move past harmful patterns. When I spoke with Cassandra, who teaches women's sacred drumming, I heard an amazing story about repeated nightmares that finally culminated with a healing moment.

"For many years," Cassandra explained, "from five years old to thirty-two, I had nightmares of hundreds and thousands of zombies and vampires running after me trying to kill me. It was terrifying and traumatic. I would be in a house and they would be all around the windows and doors, trying to pry their way in. In some dreams, I was running and they were all around. I would climb a palm tree and then the palm tree would bend to the ground where the zombies could get me. I would jump up and the tree would bend back the other way, and the zombies would still be trying to grab me. There were rules about the zombies: you don't look them in the eyes or you'll turn into one of them. You don't let them scratch you and draw blood, or bite you—or you'll turn into one of them. I never looked at them for twenty-seven years."

As Cassandra shared the story of these terrifying dreams, I felt frightened myself. Why should such a wonderful person be plagued with such painful visions? Then Cassandra told me the end of the story: "One night, after more than twenty-five years of zombie dreams, I did something different." And Cassandra described the following dream:

> *I am riding with a friend on a moped and we come up to a barricade. All the zombies are on the other side. My friend pushes some of them on the head and they fall down, but they keep coming up in droves. Then a twelve-year-old vampire comes and grabs both of my arms.*
>
> *I look her in the eyes and I begin to sing to her. The song that I sing is: "I see light behind your eyes, shining light down to my core, I see light behind your eyes, reminding me of my own shine." And as I sing this song to her, she is turning back into a little girl. Her face now has some life in it. But she is still holding on to me and starts scratching me, and I get scared. When I get scared, she turns back into a vampire.*
>
> *I think: "Oh, no—I have to keep singing to her to turn her back into a child." I want to sing*

> *but my lips are sealed. All I can do is hum to*
> *her, so I hum the song and look her in the eyes.*
> *And she turns back into a little girl. But she*
> *scratches me again and I get scared and she*
> *turns back into a vampire. I try to hum again*
> *and this time I have no voice at all.*
>
> *I think, "Great. I'll just have to silently sing to*
> *her." I look her in the eyes, and I silently sing*
> *to her. She turns back into a little girl. I wake*
> *up and never have another zombie nightmare*
> *again.*

Cassandra never questioned why the zombies came. She had simply believed she was cursed—she was accident-prone and often ill—and the dreams were part of the curse. On a deep level, she explained, she had long felt afflicted as a woman and a person of color who often experienced bigotry and exclusion. But now she felt the curse was lifted, and she no longer had to internalize society's violence. The nightmares had finally stopped.

I asked Cassandra how she had found the strength to approach the zombies and vampires with love instead of fleeing them. Cassandra told me of her journey of self-discovery, which began at age nineteen. On this spiritual journey, she encountered Dances of Universal Peace, a practice of circle-dancing with a group of people while looking into the eyes of each person to connect to the Divine within them. "The Divine in you sings to the Divine in the others. It was the first time I experienced being looked at in the eyes with love," she said. "The song I sang in the dream was in the spirit of those songs." In Cassandra's own work as a musician, she began to create exercises where people slowly learned to look one another in the eyes and bless each other.

As I listened to Cassandra's story, I understood that she had brought the practice of loving witness that she had learned from

Dances of Universal Peace into her dreams. This was the practice she drew on to show the vampire child love instead of fear. Even as Cassandra began to lose her faculties of speech, she strove to love the vampire child, who was in some way herself, as a cursed being—the way she had once thought of herself. She became the Presence in the dream, offering healing love. She was no longer a person who felt she was cursed; rather, she was a source of blessing for others, full of empowered compassion. Through her commitment to love the vampire girl, the power of the nightmare was broken.

Reflecting on how the final zombie dream changed her, Cassandra said:

> I am still learning from this dream: about oneness, about love. About loving the unlovable, loving unconditionally. She came back to being a little girl because I saw that she was just like me. We're all sons and daughters of the Divine, and I saw her and affirmed her.

Cassandra's experience shows that we can bring our learning, our healing, and our gifts back into our nightmares. Over time—maybe a lot of time—we may find the key to open the door of the dream and allow a new possibility to unfold. Continuing to attend to our dreams, even the hard ones, can help us to reach a transformative outcome.

LEARNING TO STEER:
A TALE OF FALLING AND FLYING

Sometimes our nightmares can even turn to joyful dreams. Amber, who lives in upstate New York, shared with me that she'd had recurring dreams of falling since she was seven or eight. In these frightening dreams, someone was chasing her. Fleeing, she fell through the air. She fell endlessly through many different scenes and landscapes, but never landed.

At that stage in her life, Amber was a child living in a difficult situation. She knew that her dreams reflected her inability to control the painful circumstances of her life. But later, when she was an adult, guiding her own life, Amber's falling dreams turned into flying dreams. The dreams began, as the old ones had, with a shadowy enemy behind her. Amber would begin to fly in order to flee the pursuer. Then, she would realize that she was flying and begin to take joy in it. Forgetting her pursuer and her fear, she would steer her flight to beautiful places. Usually, in these flying dreams, the scene she steered through was a great valley set within mountains. The endless passing landscapes of her nightmares had become her own version of the deep Place we find in our dreams.

Cassandra's and Amber's experiences show us how nightmares reveal our deeper truth. In that sense, nightmares are our witnesses: they are telling us our own story. Such dreams can not only show what hurts, but also be part of our healing. Amber's dream-power of joy, and Cassandra's dream-power of love, are hard-earned gifts from the dreamworld in which they struggled for so long. If we are still caught in the nightmares, we can draw hope from these stories that we too may one day find our way into the Place of Presence.

THE FIGURE ACROSS THE LAKE: FINDING GIFTS IN A NIGHTMARE

I work through nightmares in stages. I start by reflecting on the feelings that come up in the dream: a nightmare usually evokes terror, while other, less unpleasant dreams may have more mixed or confused feelings. I try to name the demon in the dream. I ask myself whether this demon has come to the dreamer personally, or whether it is an archetypal energy or a larger societal problem.

I consider whether the dream is sharing something immediate and urgent, addressing some long-standing fear, pattern, or relationship, or even diagnosing a physical ailment. And I look at whether the dream has a protective element, a resource that can offer support and help in waking life.

Paul, whose dream of deep water we explored in Chapter Three, once asked if we could take a look at a recurring childhood nightmare.

> I am part of a group descending into a dark canyon. A tour guide with a loud voice is leading us. As we descend, it gets darker and darker until the surroundings are pitch-black. As I look around I see several pairs of "eyes" floating in the blackness; the eyes are white disks without pupils. As one pair of eyes comes closer, the "tour guide" shouts, "KISS IT!" in a harsh voice. Everyone else disappears and I am suddenly left alone facing the eyes. Very frightened, I obediently, slowly approach the pair of eyes, or maybe they approach me. I can't run. I can't see anything except the eyes, which come closer and closer.
>
> There is a sudden change of scene. Surrounded by loud and startling noises like fireworks explosions, I am walking by myself down the aisle of a small grocery store. I leave the store and walk alongside a lake that looks like a millpond. A house, a sawmill-like structure, painted red, is across the lake.

The dream begins like an "underground temple" dream. Paul descends into a canyon, and we expect he may come to the Place.

Yet instead, he discovers a terrifying sight: eyes in the dark. Paul approaches the eyes and, as in many nightmares, finds he cannot run away. I wondered if the eyes under the earth might be connected to the earth and to Presence, but when I asked if Paul could imagine anything benevolent or awe-inspiring about this being, he demurred. "I couldn't imagine intimacy with it," he said. The being evoked terror and revulsion. It was clearly a dream demon.

The dream recurred several times over Paul's childhood, beginning during a difficult time when his strict military father had just returned from a war. Paul was expected to be affectionate with his father, even though he didn't feel close to this relative stranger who had been away from home for so long. Paul felt the scary entities with the eyes, and the command to "kiss it," might reflect those early moments of unfamiliarity with his father.

The dream always brought Paul to the grocery store, where he could hear and feel loud booms from exploding fireworks, and then to the quiet lake. Paul noted that his grandfather operated a red-painted sawmill out west; in fact, Paul had this dream at least twice while staying with his grandparents. It seemed that Paul was traveling in the dream to a place where he felt comfort.

I began to wonder about the connection between the two scenes, and how the store and sawmill might be resources for Paul. We began to explore the grocery store. I asked if the firework sounds he heard in the store were frightening and Paul said yes, somewhat—they were startling but not terrifying. It was as if the demon was still there, but farther away. Paul noted feeling alone in the weirdly empty grocery store and said that was why he went outside, to look for someone. A light bulb went on in my head.

I asked Paul if, in the dream, he was aware that he was looking for a caretaker to comfort him. He said yes. "Could you imagine someone coming to you from across the lake?" I asked. "I did see someone," he replied, surprised. "In the dream, there was a shadowy figure there across the lake." He had not spoken of this figure before. When I asked him to visualize that "someone" coming toward him, he saw his mother coming to embrace him. "It would be joyful for me," he said, when I asked how it would feel to have his mother embrace him. "I would get teary and cry." Paul's mother's love was the gift he had been seeking within the nightmare.

Sometimes, like Paul, we find that within the nightmare is its healing. Sometimes, even a relentlessly scary dream can teach us something crucial or offer us resources we didn't know we had. Nightmares are hard to have, but they are not "bad dreams." They are, as the Talmud says, a peek behind the curtain.

As we've noted, nightmares can be healing dreams. While healing dreams often feel good, nightmares generally don't, so we have to think about them a little differently.

If you've had a nightmare, recognize that it's a powerful and stressful event. If possible, give yourself a little time and space to recover. Have a cup of tea or a warm shower. If you've woken up in the middle of the night, turn on the light or otherwise change the context so the terror from the dream doesn't linger. But also, write down the dream and note the feelings that came up, and any associations to what you saw, heard, or felt.

When you start feeling into the nightmare, ask yourself where the demon in the dream is. Then, ask yourself where the healing resources are. In your dream, there might be a place, a friend, an animal, or a plant that brings you strength—like the figure across the lake in Paul's nightmare. Or you might find that the healing comes from within you, like the song Cassandra sang to the vampire girl. Or it might be that you wake up from the nightmare without any sense of what your resources are—in which case, you can brainstorm what your resources might be in the waking world. The next night, you can ask for another dream to clarify the first.

As with other healing dreams, try to consider what the nightmare might be telling you about an issue in your waking life. If you feel able to do some visualization or journaling, you can ask the dream demon its reasons for coming to you. Find out if it is revealing something to you, or if, like Cassandra's vampire girl, it just needs love. Or, try this: visualize the nightmare image—the demon—and then the comforting element in the dream.[7]

Notice what feelings arise. Do this several times and see if anything more becomes clear.

Don't obsess about nightmares as omens—but if you do think your nightmare might be a literal warning, keep that possibility in mind in the days and years ahead. I have had nightmares of slimy crocodiles alert me to bacterial infections. Others I know have dreamt of car accidents that occurred years later; their dream experience told them what to do to avoid getting hurt. You never know how your own nightmares might be rescuing you—or teaching you to rescue yourself.

If you're having recurring nightmares and you want them to stop, it may help to set a nightly intention for the nightmares to shift. Ask for loving, empowering dreams. And it may also help to work on whatever waking-life issue the dreams seem to be pointing to.

For example, you could use a traditional Jewish bedtime prayer that reads, in the Hebrew:

בָּרוּךְ אַתָּה ה' אֱלֹהֵינוּ מֶלֶךְ הָעוֹלָם הַמַּפִּיל
חֶבְלֵי שֵׁנָה עַל עֵינַי וּתְנוּמָה עַל עַפְעַפָּי:
וִיהִי רָצוֹן מִלְּפָנֶיךָ ה' אֱלֹהַי וֵאלֹהֵי אֲבוֹתַי
וְאִמּוֹתַי שֶׁתַּשְׁכִּיבֵנִי לְשָׁלוֹם וְתַעֲמִידֵנִי
לְשָׁלוֹם וְאַל יְבַהֲלוּנִי רַעְיוֹנַי וַחֲלוֹמוֹת רָעִים
וְהִרְהוּרִים רָעִים וּתְהֵא מִטָּתִי שְׁלֵמָה לְפָנֶיךָ
וְהָאֵר עֵינַי פֶּן אִישַׁן הַמָּוֶת כִּי אַתָּה הַמֵּאִיר
לְאִישׁוֹן בַּת עָיִן: בָּרוּךְ אַתָּה ה' הַמֵּאִיר
לְעוֹלָם כֻּלּוֹ בִּכְבוֹדוֹ.[8]

In the above prayer, God is described as masculine. If you prefer to use Hebrew in which God is feminine, you can use this version:

בְּרוּכָה אַתְּ שְׁכִינָה אֱלֹהֵינוּ רוּחַ הָעוֹלָם
הַמַּפִּילָה חֶבְלֵי שֵׁנָה עַל עֵינַי וּתְנוּמָה עַל

עַפְעַפָּי: וִיהִי רָצוֹן מִלְפָנֶיךָ שְׁכִינָה אֱלֹהַי
וֵאלֹהֵי הוֹרַי שֶׁתַּשְׁכִּיבֵנִי לְשָׁלוֹם וְתַעֲמִידֵנִי
לְשָׁלוֹם וְאַל יְבַהֲלוּנִי רַעְיוֹנַי וַחֲלוֹמוֹת רָעִים
וְהִרְהוּרִים רָעִים וּתְהֵא מִטָּתִי שְׁלֵמָה
לְפָנֶיךָ וְהָאִירִי עֵינַי פֶּן אִישַׁן הַמָּוֶת כִּי
אַתְּ הַמֵּאִירָה לְאִישׁוֹן בַּת עָיִן: בְּרוּכָה אַתְּ
שְׁכִינָה הַמֵּאִירָה לְעוֹלָם כֻּלּוֹ בִּכְבוֹדָהּ.[9]

Blessed are You, Eternal Presence,
Guide of the Cosmos, who closes
my eyes in sleep and my eyelids in
slumber. May it be Your will, Source
of Life whom my ancestors honored
and whom I honor, to lay me down
in peace and raise me up in peace.
May no troubling thoughts upset
me, no evil dreams. May my bed be
peaceful and whole in Your sight,
and may You keep me in life, for You
are the giver of revelations. Blessed
are You, who enlightens the whole
world with Your Presence.

You might also repeat these words from an eighteenth-
century Sephardic incantation (originally composed in
Ladino) for peaceful sleep:

> *Me echo en mi kama,*
> *de Miryam a-nevia*
> *me kovijo kon kolcha*
> *de rey Shelomo*
> *entrego mi alma*
> *en poder del Kriador:*
> *El ke me la guadre*

de fuego de flama,
de muerte de hapetanya.
Sero mis puertas i mis ventanas
kon siyo del rey Shelomo meleh
Mihael de mi derecha,
Gavriel de mi estiedra,
Shehina pozada sovre mi kavesa.

I lie down in my bed
protected by Miriam the prophetess;
I am covered with the quilt
of Solomon the king.
I give up my soul to God's power.
May God keep it safe
from flames of fire
and from sudden death.
I close my doors and windows
with King Solomon's seal.
Michael is on my right hand
and Gabriel on my left
and the Presence above my head.[10]

CHAPTER 9

Dreaming the Sacred Union

Then the Tree of Life and all the trees of the
Garden of Eden emit sweet odors, and praise
their Source, for the Lady is preparing Herself
to enter under the canopy, to unite Herself
with Her Spouse . . . in perfect love without
separation.

    —Zohar[1]

The Presence can come to us in just about any form. Yet some traditions, from kabbalah to Catholic mysticism to the Hindu philosophies, say the most intimate experience we can have with that Being is as a beloved. In the kabbalah, Shekhinah often appears as a lover. She arrives on Friday night as the Sabbath bride, as the liturgy celebrates her: "Come, dear one, to greet the bride—let us welcome the face of the Sabbath."[2] The Beloved may also be a bridegroom, as when the kabbalists say: "The Sabbath night is the joy of the Queen with the King, and their uniting."[3]

This image of the Divine or the universe as a beloved can arise in our dreams as well. Indeed, these can be some of the most potent dreams we have. In such a dream, we might find ourselves in a love relationship or an erotic embrace. We might be the bride or bridegroom at the wedding. Or we might have an enchanting, immersive encounter of some other kind. We might say these dream moments are a celebration of our unity with the cosmic oneness. We are not only part of the web of being; we are needed and wanted, embraced and aroused. Rodger Kamenetz teaches that sacred encounters "of very deep feeling and sensuality" are at the heart of our journey into the temple of our dreams.[4] Such dream experiences are related to what David Abram calls the "felt encounter between our sensate body and the animate earth."[5]

The unification of beings across worlds is sometimes referred to as the sacred marriage. In ancient Greece, it was called *hieros gamos*; in Christian tradition, it is sometimes called *unio mystica*. Kabbalists use the term *yichud* to refer to the loving union of the Holy One and the Shekhinah, a union that connects all worlds and pours out blessings on the cosmos. Indian Vaishnava philosophy names the Source as Rama or Bihari, meaning "the supreme enjoyer (of creation),"[6] for the Source not only loves but enjoys us as creations. The sacred marriage is a union between God and the soul, between humans and the realm of spirit. Some ancient cultures (such as pre-Christian Ireland and ancient Sumer) used the ritual of sacred marriage to confirm a king.[7] Shamanic practitioners from Africa to Siberia are sometimes understood to be married to a god or spirit.[8] Catholic nuns have long been called "brides of Christ."

Union with a dream lover can invite us to joyfully embrace our oneness with the cosmos in a way that is tender, healing, nourishing, and empowering. Sacred union dreams help us heal wounds and ruptures related to self-worth and loneliness, allowing us to transcend old patterns of isolation and self-doubt. These healing dream unions can alchemically change us.

In Chapter One, we considered how the Presence in dreams offers us images of a conscious Being underlying reality, and how that Being calls us forth to awareness and communion. It brings us healing so that we can unblock or unconfuse ourselves, clearing anything that interferes with our experience of that oneness. Sacred union dreams are, in a sense, the ultimate expression of this process.

We are an organic particle of a vast living cosmos that we can barely comprehend—yet in a sacred union dream, we merge in joyful union with that vastness, which also seeks connection with us. This kind of dream works on a level of physical love, and on a transcendent level, in which we come to understand the preciousness of what and who we are. We don't need to feel small in the face of the universe; we are partners with it, entwined in loving and pleasurable contact.

THE TREASURE:
DREAMS OF MEETING THE BELOVED

Amelie is a sacred musician and kohenet. Her dream of the sacred union is a beautiful rendering of what it means to meet the Beloved in a dream.

> *I'm outside and there are people scattered about. Everyone is anxiously and competitively*

*looking for treasure. I go over to the stump of a
tree and notice that inside is a circular box, like
a hatbox. I take it out, knowing I don't have to
hide it, even though I know this is the treasure
everyone is looking for. I know that, whatever it is, they won't want it. They won't know
its value, because they are looking for gold or
diamonds.*

*Inside the box is a mirror. I hold up the mir-
ror, and inside I see that I am a young woman. There are people inside the mirror world,
and they are down a hallway, and they are calling me. They are calling me because I am the
queen and it is my wedding night. I go through
the mirror into their world. They are excited for
me to open a door, and inside will be my groom.
I do. He is there, waiting for me, lying on his
side on a bed, a beautiful young man.*

In my reading of this dream, the mirror in the dream has a double
meaning. It is a mirror reflecting Amelie's true nature as the bride
of the Beloved, allowing her to experience and identify this true
nature. And like Alice's looking glass, the mirror is also a portal
to the deeper world, the world of the unconscious, where unity
with the All can occur. In this world, Amelie experiences herself as
the Queen, the Presence Herself. The Presence is within us, is us—
we manifest Her/Him/They/It just as everything around us does.

When Amelie had this dream, she had no idea of the kabbalistic myth of the Divine Bride and Bridegroom joining together.
A day later, she was astonished to discover she had dreamt this
myth. She writes: "The day after this dream, a friend invited me
to a Shabbat dinner. At the meal, people spoke about the Shabbat
queen. I had little to no reference for that; I had never observed

Shabbat, nor did I have any knowledge about its symbols. The conversation caused me to remember the dream, and I told the people at the table. We were all stunned."

In the world of our imagination, and especially in the dream-world, we naturally intuit mythic images and relationships. Amelie's entry into the otherworld to be wed is a unique iteration of an ancient experience that countless mystics have cherished. It is also a call to greater self-love and connection with the world. As poet Dare Sohei writes: "We will all suffer some pain, we will all die, and yet everyone can feel loved, if not by other humans, [then] by joy, by music or by the pervading gaze of the forest."[9] The love we receive in dreams and other experiences of merging with the Presence does not depend on having a partner or developing a romantic crush. It is more akin to immersing in the ocean: an overwhelming joy at being interwoven.

MARRYING THE DRAGON:
THE POWER OF SACRED UNION
DREAMS

Of course, a sacred union dream doesn't have to be a heterosexual pairing. In this beautiful dream, I found myself partnered with a female dragon:

> *A dragon lifts me up into the air and holds me in a dazzling, sparkling cloud. I cannot exactly see the dragon but I know she is there, and I know that what we are doing is making love. The union between us is happening on the in-side of my body rather than the outside. I am amazed, in awe, delighted.*

The dragon, a misty, out-of-focus, fiery being, lifts me up and joins with my body—yet somehow this joining happens not in any of the usual ways but rather inside me, pervading my entire body. The lovemaking happens inside my cells, and it brings me incomprehensible delight. I viscerally feel that the Presence loves and desires me, and She is everywhere, even inside me.

Sacred union dreams are marked by the transformative feelings, like bliss and peace, that arise in response to the union. These feelings stay with the dreamer upon awakening, and can then be recalled when the dreamer meets the cosmos in the waking world. Perhaps some of the other dreams we've looked at involving interactions with the Presence can also be interpreted romantically. For example, interactions with elements and guides can bring us this feeling. Sometimes the dream teaches us how to find this union in waking life. We can experience bliss, awe, and joy in contemplating a dandelion or a puddle, in seeing the face of a friend, in holding hands with a partner. Once we know the feeling of the *hieros gamos*, the holy wedding, we can find it almost anywhere.

DIVING DEEP:
SACRED UNION AND THE EARTH

As we have noted throughout the book, the Presence also manifests as Place. Sometimes our sacred connection is not with an entity but with the elements themselves. The Presence can manifest as earth, sky, water, or fire. Finding ourselves in relationship with these elements can also be a sacred marriage.

Seth, a rabbi, has participated in a men's dream circle for many years and has worked with a variety of dream counselors. When I told him I was writing this book, he offered me one of his dreams to consider—a sacred union dream, in a subtle way.

> *I am in a store that sells books of maps, some of which have beautiful photographs of the places on the maps. One of these map books is con-*

> *nected to a well-known scholar of Jewish philos-*
> *ophy and the Bible. I have bought one road map*
> *and am buying another that includes wonderful*
> *photographs: black-and-white photos of various*
> *scenes with mountains going down into lakes*
> *and oceans. I buy this book despite imagining*
> *that my wife might criticize me. Then I am at*
> *a bagel store and buy bagels, but leave them*
> *in the store.*

The mountains in the map-photographs slope down into oceans—a descent to the underground temple. One of the maps in particular is "associated" with a wise scholar who studies sacred books, suggesting that the sacred book and the sacred earth are one and the same. Bagels sometimes mark a contemporary cultural Jewish identity, a surface identity which Seth leaves behind as he heads for the deeper mysteries:

> *I am walking with my wife and cousin in a*
> *beautiful area that I have seen pictures of in*
> *the book I just bought. They ask me if I want to*
> *walk alone, and I say that they can come if they*
> *want. The landscape of this place is mountains*
> *and hillsides of dark sand that slope down to a*
> *beach. There are abandoned and half-torn-down*
> *buildings on the hillsides. It is a beautiful*
> *place, open to the sky.*
>
> *We walk along together and then come to a hill-*
> *top. Down below are rolling hills of sand and a*
> *path that goes down to the ocean. I am wearing*
> *only my bathing suit and I ask them if they*
> *want to go and swim. They say, "No, you go,"*
> *and I start running down the path. I pass a*

> *man who is also heading down to the beach. He*
> *looks at ease in this place, as if it is a second*
> *home for him.*

Seth had feared his wife would criticize him for buying the maps; perhaps he was concerned that she wouldn't approve of him taking a solo journey. He invites his companions along, but in the end, they support him going on this journey into the deep waters alone.

Seth comments: "The man I pass on the way down the path to the beach is very comfortable in this place, the way I want to be." This man may be the wise scholar of the maps—or perhaps Seth is seeing a version of himself that is completely comfortable with his immersion in the Great Deep.

The dream continues:

> *I have a few quarters in my pocket and am*
> *wearing my wedding ring, which I usually take*
> *off when I swim in a lake or ocean. I don't want*
> *to take the time to go back and leave my ring,*
> *so I just keep running to the water.*
>
> *The sun is low enough to make the water*
> *sparkle. The wind is blowing so there are small*
> *waves that carry the sparkles along toward me*
> *as I dive into the water. The water is cool and*
> *refreshing. I dive deep down and swim, and*
> *then come back to the dock. I get out of the*
> *water and feel renewed.*

Seth notes: "I do not take my wedding ring off or get rid of the money in my pocket; I do not have to abandon materiality and relationships in order to live a spiritual life." Seth is right. Yet perhaps both the wedding ring and the coins have even deeper implications.

The wedding ring may suggest that Seth is going to be "married" via his entry into the ocean. The coins may imply a kind of death; in Greek myth, a soul who wanted to cross the river Styx into the underworld needed coins to pay the boatman. Seth's dive into the waters is the moment of his marriage with the cosmos. He reemerges and swims back to the dock, refreshed and joyful.

> *Later, I call the bagel store to see if they have my bagels that I have left there so I can go and pick them up. They don't understand what I am talking about so I have to explain what has happened until they remember.*

The bagel quest at the end of the dream injects a humorous quality: this is a scene we might find in a Seinfeld episode. Yet those who are accustomed to spirit journeys—shamans and sacred practitioners—tell us that food is grounding after a journey. Seth's attempt to reclaim his bagels reflects his returning to the human world, with all of its social signals and physical needs. We might say Seth returns from primordial union and picks up his public persona. It is Seth, not the store staff, who needs to remember what has happened in his previous life. So too, whenever we dive deep and merge into elemental Being, we must ultimately return to ourselves.

YOU ARE NOT ALONE

In sacred union dreams, we are often in deep, loving relationships—whether these are sexual or not. Often such dreams are medicine for our core psychological and emotional wounds. Very simply, such dreams help us to feel loved.

Here is a dream of mine that affected me greatly:

I have been traveling a long time, and am telling a friend about my travels. I am describing how God said to me: "I am going to give you a gift. I am going to give you wings so you can fly." I describe to my friend how I became angry and said, "God, what good are wings? No one will listen to me because I have wings. Everyone will just think that I am strange. Why are you giving me wings?" But God said: "You will see. People will listen to you."

Then, as I finish this story, I look at one of my moles; it has a foot-long hair poking out of it. I think: "How did I let it get that long?" I try to cut it off with scissors and it turns into a feather with a strong shaft. It bleeds when I try to cut it. More feathers grow. I know it is true, I am going to be able to fly.

In the next scene, I am saying goodbye to a friend with red hair. He is going on a boat. I ask him not to leave, and tell him I am sad that he is going. He tells me that wherever he goes he will always be with me. He tells me that he has been through many lives with me. He even tells me how I died in some of those lives. He tells me not to be afraid because we can never be separated.

This dream is painfully on target. It touches a core wound in my life: my sense of difference and my sense of loneliness, both of which began when I was a bright, creative, and rather odd little girl growing up in suburbia. I was often picked on, ignored, disregarded, and mocked. I had such a desire to give of myself, yet my gifts seemed to alienate others and drive them away. In the dream, I am still carrying that sad and frightened view of myself. If I am not ordinary, I think, then other people will reject me. Because of this fear, I reject myself: my own gifts, my own being. "No one will listen to me because I have wings," I say.

The dream then reveals to me an image: a feather that grows out of my body. I try to cut the feather off, but it is part of me, and it bleeds when I try to remove it. I cannot escape who I am: more feathers are already growing. The wings are part of me, and I cannot excise them without doing irreparable harm to myself. I have wings, whether I want them or not. With this new understanding, I can never return to the cramped reality I inhabited before.

In the dream's next scene, I meet a dream beloved with red hair. As if in answer to the fear I expressed earlier in the dream—the fear that no one will listen to me, no one will love me—he offers me undying love. More than that, my beloved offers me knowledge of my forgotten past: he knows even the parts of me that I do not know myself, including our enduring love throughout numerous lifetimes. I do not need to be afraid, the dream lover says. My connection to Presence transcends space and time, life and death.

At the end of the dream, the beloved is departing on a ship—bound, perhaps, for the otherworld. I am sad, at the end of the dream, to be separated from my love. But I still have the wings, and I have the assurance that the separation is temporary: I am never really alone.

I still think of that dream, at moments when I feel lonely, or on days when I feel like I can't do anything right. I still remember how loved I felt, even at the moment when the lover's boat departed and I woke up. This dream effected a transformation: I was able to experience myself as loved and loving, as worthwhile, with something to share with others.

SACRED UNION AS JOINING
WITH THE SELF

The sacred union that occurs in a dream can enact an alchemical transformation within the dreamer. In this dream, a woman I'll call Phoebe describes a profound encounter with a sea monster, in which she is able to leave behind years of frightening dreams:

> *I have a small houseplant shedding leaves, doing poorly. I don't know why it is dying, or how to treat it, so I ask my mother what to do. She takes the plant and removes it from its soil, exposing the root ball, and places it back in its clay pot, which she has filled with warm water. I know that I am to wait and see what happens.*
>
> *As I observe, hundreds of tiny organisms emerge from the plant. They weep liquid from the plant's core out to the bark and drip like sticky neon-green tears into the water. The water begins to swarm with activity and one of the creatures rapidly develops before my eyes. Its color darkens to a mottled brown camouflage, its dorsal fin cutting the surface of the water. It has a large anvil-shaped head which tapers into a stubby tail: the shape of a truncated eel.*
>
> *When it grows to the size of the pot, its head emerges from the water with gaping jaws, swiveling around on the whirlpool of its tail. I take the creature in hand, scoop it out of the water by its tail, and insert it unceremoniously into my vagina.*

The creature integrates with me. My body sub-
sumes its identity, until it is fully incorporated
into my womb. Then, my womb becomes gold,
and my whole body becomes gold. The gold
emanates upward through my whole body, from
the hips, up through my rib cage, breasts and
heart, through the expansion of my upraised
arms, throat and head. Gold light radiates
through my pelvic floor, through the crown of my
head, and surrounds me in an ever-expanding
halo. I am illuminated with gold.

In reflecting on this dream, Phoebe recalls, "I have a long history of nightmares about sea monsters. In my earlier dreams, those monsters were usually much larger and more intimidating: sinuous toxic leviathans that undulate in warm perfumed lotus water. In those dreams, only I am able to detect the presence of the monster; other bathers and onlookers are attracted to the sweet smell and warm bathwater temperature of the pool. So here I am in this dream, presented with a manageable pint-sized version of my former nightmares."

By encountering and literally internalizing what previously frightened her, Phoebe has been healed of her fears and released from her nightmares. She has become one with what seemed to threaten her before. And not only this, but she has attained a glorious, powerful state in which she radiates light into the world.

We might compare Phoebe's dream to the Hindu myth called the Devi Mahatmya (the story of the Navaratri holiday). In this story, the Goddess must save the world from the demon Raktabija. Every time she tries to slice him apart, new demons sprout from every drop of his blood. The only way she can destroy him is to drink every drop of blood and absorb the demons into her body.[10] Like the myth, Phoebe's dream suggests that we can overcome what we fear, not by othering it, but by integrating it.

This kind of sacred union dream offers an alchemical healing—a healing that transforms the whole self. Alchemists call this *coniunctio*, a union of opposing forces that leads to something entirely new. The alchemist Gerhard Dorn understood *coniunctio* as a state in which "two are made one."[11] So too, the sacred marriage can offer us integration of the fragmented parts of our lives.

If you have had a dream with themes of love, sex, union, or connection, see if it feels right to think of it as a moment of love and desire sent to you from the universe. If your sacred union was with a person you know, it might mean that person's love is important for you right now—or, it might mean that the Presence has clothed itself in that person for a moment to express the love of the Presence for you.

If you wish to develop a sustained relationship with your dream beloved, you could start by writing a letter or a poem dedicated to them, or making a regular time of the day or the week when you meditate on their presence. You can make a note of whether that being returns in another dream. And it may be wise not to get too attached to one version of your dream beloved, as their form is likely to change as you continue to dream.

Sometimes a union dream is addressing a core wound or obstacle in your life. See if there is a fear, insecurity, or resentment that the dream comes to transform. Or, sometimes the dream is inviting you into a new vision of yourself. Notice how the dream may be expanding your self-knowledge and offering you unexplored possibilities.

If in the dream you witnessed a wedding or erotic encounter but were not part of it yourself, ask yourself what the love you witnessed makes you feel or desire. Or, go back into the dream and imagine yourself as one of the lovers. See what it feels like to be part of the love at the heart of the dream.

If your sacred dream union was with a plant or animal or the earth itself, you can go out and seek immersion in the elements: go swimming in a mountain stream or spelunking in a cave. Stand on the top of a hill and feel the wind. Lie in a meadow beneath the summer sun. Accept the natural world as your lover.

If you wish, you can write a letter to the beloved in your dream, and then write their letter back to you. You can let the dream inspire art or music or poetry or a walk in the woods. You can put an image or a quote that reminds you of the dream in your home. You can think of ways to spread love in the world, in appreciation for the dream you have received.

It can be hard to believe in so much love and faith showered on us from the Presence. Sometimes our psyches begin to second-guess the dream and imagine that we are not really deserving of it. If it feels right, tell someone else and have them show you the beauty of the dream. That can be very helpful.

Kabbalists begin many prayers and rituals with a few words of intention: "For the sake of the unification of the Holy One and the Shekhinah"[12] (the transcendent masculine Divine with the immanent feminine Divine). We might perhaps go into our dreaming each night with an even simpler intention: "For the sake of sacred union . . ."

CHAPTER 10

Death and Rebirth in Dreams

Everywhere, the death, the seeds.
 —Patricia Monaghan[1]

Their end is embedded in their beginning and
their beginning in their end.
 —Sefer Yetzirah[2]

The natural world moves in cycles. Seasons come and go; creatures are born, grow up, and die; trees flower, fruit, and drop their leaves. The dreamworld, too, moves in cycles. We don't, in my experience, progress from murky dreams to enchanted ones, and stay there. Even if one night we receive dream healing from an archangel or find ourselves in a temple beneath the earth, it may not be long before we work our way back to dreams where we're lost on the subway. Dreams are not a one-way hero's journey, at least not in my experience. They ebb and flow like the tides.

Some of our most powerful dreams invite us to embrace the cycle of change and transformation, death and rebirth. These dreams may reflect endings and beginnings in our lives. They may initiate us into new ways of being—or address the great mystery of dying. Sometimes these dreams connect us to the earth's larger cycles of growth and decay, as what dies nourishes new life.

The underground temple is like a great tree, but also like a fallen log: as it decays into the earth, it nourishes realities yet to be born. Indeed, Jung says that one who enacts the cycle of death and rebirth "experiences in this way the permanence and continuity of life, which outlasts all changes of form and, phoenix-like, continually rises anew from its own ashes."[3]

The Talmud teaches that three keys are in the hands of God alone: the keys of rain, of birth, and of resurrection.[4] The processes by which death and decay become life and renewal are divine mysteries. When we encounter such processes in our dreams, we have encountered the Presence at work in the rhythms of our lives. Indeed, in the Zohar, the biblical ancestors dig their own graves, die, and are reborn every single day.[5] Perhaps this vision teaches us to embrace our own daily transformations, even the ones that scare us.

Dream scholar Karen Jaenke writes that dreams allow for a "fusion of the past and present or present and future, when new, creative possibilities arise and unfold . . . Old patterns transform in healing directions, setting new templates in the psyche that can then be ritualized and enacted in the everyday, visible world."[6] This shifting of our inner landscape is a kind of constant rebirth, just as the earth is always changing and renewing itself.

In the sixth century BCE, the prophet Ezekiel had a waking vision—or perhaps a dream—of a valley of dry bones. Instructed to prophesy over the bones, Ezekiel repeats God's promise: "I will cause breath to enter you and you shall live again."[7] Sometimes, in our dreams, we witness similar scenes. In one recent dream, a friend of mine, bike-riding on a beach, was swallowed into the sand. I called out to him and began to unearth his body. As I uncovered his face, I could feel his breathing. Perhaps, in unearthing him, I was also rebirthing myself.

ENTERING THE MYSTERY:
DREAM INITIATIONS

Initiation is a rite of passage that marks a change in our self-understanding and our role in the world. Traditionally, the young are initiated into adulthood; one can also be initiated into a spiritual tradition or a sacred calling. Those who are initiated are transformed, and cannot return to their original state. Death-and-rebirth dreams sometimes indicate that we are undergoing an initiation into a new phase of our lives.

Daniel, a rabbi and artist, shared his dream journal with me, and in it was this dream. It gave me chills when I read it.

> *A boy I know is dying—or rather, I know inside myself that he has to die. I shoot him with a gun and burn him with fire: a large blaze, like a campfire. As the boy burns, ooze comes out of the fire, melting into a primordial soup. It is messy and gross: pink, bubbly, and slimy. Then the boy is covered with a sheet. Another person*

goes to look at him lying under the sheet. He is
a pile of mush.

Then the boy rises back up. He has antlers.
He is alive. He is perfectly fine. I feel terror,
awe, and fear when I see him alive. The boy is
talking in tongues. I am dumbfounded, fright-
ened, and confused. I tell the boy he has to "let
go and leave"—I want him to go away.

One way to read the dream is that the boy is Daniel himself, and in order to grow, Daniel must kill the earlier self within him. This process is messy and unpleasant and turns the boy into "mush"; there is a dissolution of elements, a breaking down of structure. Yet impossibly, as Daniel watches, the dissolved corpse reconstitutes itself and the boy lives again, transformed into a magical being: he now has antlers and speaks in tongues.

From ancient Mesopotamia to Siberia to North America, shamans and ritual celebrants have worn antlers to represent the spirit realm since Neolithic times. Antlers may also suggest the horned Lord of the Forest in Celtic mythology. We might also add that the boy in Daniel's dream seems similar to the myths of dying and reborn gods: Osiris, Attis, Tammuz, Persephone, or Jesus. Daniel, too, is reborn with new powers, with the ability to walk in the spirit realm. This dream occurred while Daniel was in rabbinical school and perhaps indicates his integration of his sacred purpose. Rabbinical ordination is a kind of initiation—a change in identity that transforms one's whole life.

Encountering this boy, Daniel is terrified. Yet the "let go" he utters in the dream may really be a message to himself, to let go into his new self, to become the resurrected boy. In fact, Daniel felt clear that the dream was a communication that would help him become his true self: "My dreams are showing me an alternate way of existing in the mythical realm."

Yet Daniel was also concerned about his dream resistance to the deer-boy. As we discussed the impact of the dream, he asked me: "How do you begin to harness the potential [of the dream] when you've told the spirit guide: 'Go away?'" I suggested that he could go back into the dream to meet the boy again, to ask him what message he brought, what he was asking Daniel to do.

Reflecting on the dream, Daniel reached a profound insight: "I want to move into a place of surrender to the unknown. Yet I always fight and resist." But the fear is only a superficial layer on top of Daniel's true desire, which he now states clearly: "I want to become that boy." The deer-boy shows Daniel that releasing his earlier ways of thinking and being may be scary, but will allow him to fully enter his new powers.

CHRYSALIS DREAMING:
FROM GRAVE TO WOMB

Another initiation dream comes from Gracia, a psychotherapist living in Spain. Gracia spoke to me at a time when she was having strong spiritual experiences and feeling called to work with the sacred feminine.

> *I know that I am going to die, and I am scared. In order to slow down the dying process, I am being wrapped in a gauzy white fabric from head to toe. I am deposited in a narrow canal in the earth. Then I am covered with soil. I know my husband is there watching over me while this is happening. There is a dwelling made of wood nearby.*
>
> *There is a star in the sky that is very bright. I can perceive the passage of time because the star moves across the sky. The sky changes*

> *color to a dark teal. As the star accompanies*
> *me across the sky, I am comforted.*
>
> *Suddenly I am brought back and unwrapped. I*
> *feel relief and renewal. My husband is there and*
> *is very old. His skin is wrinkled. He has been*
> *there waiting. I have not aged. I am shocked by*
> *how old he is.*

Gracia, dying in her dream, finds herself wrapped in a gauzy fabric. She resembles a caterpillar within a chrysalis, and is covered with soil like a seed. These images are dreamspeak for radical change. The narrow, vagina-like canal is the doorway to the underground temple. Just as the ancients created passage tombs, ritually treating the earth as a place where death could turn to life, Gracia enters the belly of the earth to be reborn. The dream also intimates the earth's power to turn death into life through decay and growth.

Indigenous spiritual practitioners and healers are sometimes initiated by becoming deathly ill, by being buried in the earth, or by undergoing a similar death-like experience. We might say Gracia, too, is undergoing an initiation through the dream. Gracia is not alone in this initiatory experience. She has two guardians: her husband, who watches over her and dwells in the little hut near her womb-tomb, and a bright star above her, moving across the sky to show her that time is passing.

When the dreamer is unwrapped from her chrysalis, she is astonished by how much time has passed. Her husband has aged, though she has not. This part of the dream conjures up many myths and stories: people who dance with the fairies for what feels like a night, only to discover they've been away for decades; or Rip Van Winkle, who falls asleep and wakes up a generation later; or the Talmudic character Honi, who sleeps under a tiny sapling and awakes to find himself an old man and the sapling a massive tree.[8]

It might also suggest the myth of Eos, goddess of the dawn, who loved the human Tithonus and made him immortal, but found her plan had gone awry when her husband aged into a shriveled grasshopper.[9]

As noted above, Gracia had this dream at a time when she was trying to understand how to incorporate her newfound devotion to the divine feminine into her work as a psychotherapist. The dream seemed to be offering her an initiation via burial in the earth. I asked Gracia to reenter this dream in a meditative state, and speak with her guardians: her husband and the star.

Her husband offered her love and support. And when Gracia spoke to the star, it offered her an image of a hand with a stalk of grain. Gracia was astonished when I told her the image of a hand holding a stalk of grain was at the center of the Greek mysteries of regeneration, the Eleusinian Mysteries of Demeter and Persephone. In Gracia's re-visioning of the dream, she had re-intuited the ancient Greek belief that we are like the grain, capable of death and rebirth.

When I asked Gracia to feel the results of her rebirth in her body, she said: "My hips are bigger," implying a new readiness to be a "birthgiver," a creator. When I asked her what she saw at the end of the dream, she said: "A whole village is waiting for me."

DEATH AND THE BRIDEGROOM:
MARRYING THE PRESENCE

Many spiritual traditions understand dying as a moment when we merge with divinity. For example, the Sufi tradition refers to death as the "wedding," and when someone has died, one says that they have "wedded the Beloved." We may also feel the spiritual experience of merging with the Presence through meditation or prayer as a kind of death. The Chasidic masters call it *bitul hayesh*, the nullification of self. Sometimes death-and-rebirth dreams hint at these mysteries of communion between human and Divine.

This dream of death, rebirth, and wedding the Presence was offered by Eli, a kabbalah scholar.

I'm in an elevator with other people. We are going down. The lights on the control panel are off. People start pressing the buttons frantically, but it's clear that the controls are not working and we're going to crash. There's a moment when everyone panics, and then—we do crash, and we do die.

I'm dead, but I still seem to be in the world, walking around. I'm talking to a friend, and it's clear that this person can see me and hear me. I say, "Can you also feel me?" and I shake their hand; it turns out I still have a physical presence. That's reassuring, but I can feel that I am only going to be in the world a little while longer.

I decide that I should do some teaching while I still have time. I think to myself that I should teach about yeridah letzorekh aliyah *(descending in order to ascend) because this is a kabbalistic concept accessible to many people. I decide to teach it at the synagogue where I taught my first kabbalah class many years ago.*

Once I arrive at the synagogue, I walk down a long corridor, or maybe descend to a lower level, to find the room where I am teaching. When I open the door, I'm astonished to see a big banquet table where people dressed all in white are singing Jewish songs. And I think: "I didn't

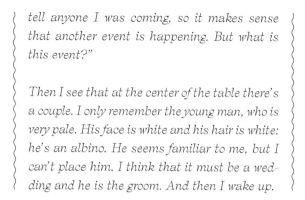

tell anyone I was coming, so it makes sense that another event is happening. But what is this event?"

Then I see that at the center of the table there's a couple. I only remember the young man, who is very pale. His face is white and his hair is white: he's an albino. He seems familiar to me, but I can't place him. I think that it must be a wedding and he is the groom. And then I wake up.

A striking element in the dream is the phrase *yeridah letzorekh aliyah,* "descent for the sake of ascent," a kabbalistic phrase that refers to moving farther away from the Divine (often into the underworld or a place of evil) in order to generate more holiness or deeper connection upon one's return. We might relate this concept to the way the soul "descends" from heaven to earth in order to fulfill its spiritual potential, thus "ascending" to a higher state. Similarly, in kabbalistic sources, Shekhinah "descends" into the material world in order to elevate physical substance and bring it closer to the divine realms.

We know that such "descent" is the theme here because, at the beginning of the dream, the elevator "descends" abruptly and crashes. Eli believes he's dead, but remains in a kind of liminal state in which he still has all the attributes of being alive. Sensing he has limited time, he decides to teach about the mystical concept of *yeridah letzorekh aliyah*—because this is one of his areas of expertise, but also perhaps because *this is the journey he is on.* Through these words, the dream has let the dreamer know that his "descent" in the elevator is for the purpose of a greater ascent to come.

As we have learned already, the kabbalah often depicts the union of the ethereal with the physical realms as a wedding. It may be that the bridegroom Eli sees is his soul, marrying Shekhinah.

Or perhaps he has become Shekhinah, and he is the bride arriving to wed the Holy One of Blessing embodied in the bridegroom (since the bride is not otherwise apparent in the scene). Either way, this wedding is the *aliyah*, the ascent, for which Eli descended in the elevator.

It may be that Eli is dreaming of the union with the Presence that will come after his death. His own mother had recently died at the time of the dream, so mortality was on his mind. Or perhaps he is dreaming of his birth—his soul descending from hidden worlds into a mortal existence. What is clear is that the dream shows Eli that he does not only teach about the sacred union: he is part of it. His life is a *yeridah letzorekh aliyah*, a descent for the sake of ascent.

Eli's question "Can you feel me?" reminds him and us that being human is about being embodied, and being in relationship. This may ultimately be the most powerful question of the dream: How can we authentically be felt by others and feel them in return?

THE EARTH AS AGENT OF REBIRTH

We have already seen, in Gracia's dream, the earth's power to generate life from death. In this dream, told to me by Miriam, a divinity student, the earth holds the power to heal the wounds of the dreamer, and to end enmity and violence.

> *I am in some kind of war, I think World War II. I am a man in the dream, but I am also myself—it is as if I am viewing someone else's experience from within their body. I am a German soldier, lying facedown on a battlefield, pretending to be dead so the approaching enemy won't shoot me. But a British soldier comes up behind me and shoots me in the back. As*

the bullet tears into my back, I ask the earth to support me, to absorb the injury, to permeate my body with peace and healing, to filter the pain out of me. I am worried I will harm or burden the earth with my request, but then I understand that the earth can use and transform the energy. I am a lightning rod between the violence of war and the earth.

I don't die, but I can't move. A second British soldier comes and shoots me again. Again I ask for help from the earth, and again I feel peace and healing washing over me, and again I don't die. Then the British soldiers who had been walking near me come under attack. One of them gets shot and collapses on top of me. I can tell he is in immense pain and that he thinks he is going to die. He thinks I am a dead body, but I gasp in a big breath of air and he is startled and rolls off of me.

We are both lying belly-down in the mud, wounded, and facing each other. I take his hand and breathe with him, and try to act as a conduit to filter his pain into the earth, the same way I did with mine. We feel healing and life essence flowing through us. I continue to be the lightning rod, silently encouraging him to not absorb the pain himself and instead to transfer it through me to the earth, where it will be washed and transformed into energy again.

In a little while his comrades come to get him to take him to their hospital, but he won't loosen

his grip on my hand. As his friends pull him
across the field, I easily slide along with them,
holding hands with the wounded soldier. They
pull us to safety and we lie next to each other in
a sort of open-air field hospital for a long time,
trying to recover.

As a wounded soldier, utterly vulnerable, Miriam comes to understand that the earth can transform the energy of violence and use it for other purposes. Then Miriam finds she is able to do for an "enemy" soldier what she has done for herself. The former adversaries become linked, both of them having been saved by the earth's healing ability.

Miriam writes: "I've been involved in leftist radical politics and activism, but have grown increasingly uncomfortable with how much the movements I've been involved with demonize 'the other.' I've been feeling more and more the importance of bridging the distance between myself and those with differing ideologies through compassion and deep listening." The dream offers Miriam wisdom for her activist work: "I was struck by the feeling of surrender and of following my intuition. The fact that I was nonviolent and a healing presence throughout the dream saved me and others. The idea of standing my ground without arming myself felt powerful." This wisdom can now inform Miriam's work and life.

Miriam's dream also offers her the practice of "earthing" as a way of healing wounds. This is a message for all of us. The earth is always recycling its materials, repurposing plant and animal matter to feed other organisms and create new soil—even absorbing and transforming human-made toxins. For instance, mycelium can be used to clean pollutants.[10] Mangroves can protect shorelines and filter heavy metals.[11] In a phenomenon called rewilding, nature has actually been able to reabsorb urban infrastructure and return to wilderness.[12] While pollution can sometimes overwhelm nature, the earth does have the ability to heal and renew itself. Indeed, the concept of resurrection or rebirth derives from our embodied experience of the earth and its cycles, in which death gives rise to life and destruction paves the way for restoration.

Intuiting this, many ancient rituals use earth, fire, wind, or water to physically and spiritually cleanse and transform.[13] If we listen carefully, our dreams will tell us which elements we need to recharge: water, earth, trees, stones, fresh air, etc. Miriam's dream, for example, prescribes establishing a simple connection to the earth as a way to heal and pacify ourselves and one another.

DREAMS OF THE DYING

While we may dream of death even when we are not physically dying, it is also true that dreams help us cope with our losses, hopes, fears, and questions as we approach our mortality. Mary Jo Heyen, a dreamworker who works in hospice care, notes that people who are dying have normal dreams even several weeks before their death. However, a few days before death, people often experience "supportive presences and visions."[14] It seems the Presence manifests in a special way to those who are transitioning between life and death. Heyen affirms that it is crucial to pay attention to these dreams and not treat them as hallucinations or as something to be afraid of. Dreams are a gift to the dying, guiding them on their journey.

Patricia Bulkley, a hospice dreamworker, reports this recurring dream from Ruth, who was dying. Ruth had been struggling because her Christian faith, which had been a central part of her life, no longer seemed to mean anything to her. Now that she was dying, her faith had evaporated: "It didn't seem possible that God could be captured in any earthly frame of reference." Instead, she felt drawn to the idea of God as a "creative Presence." She felt she had "lost it all," and was experiencing deep shame. Her hospice dreamworker encouraged her to explore her new ideas and consider that she might not have lost faith, but rather might be going through a "faith transformation." A few days later, Ruth had this dream:

> There were several huge deep blue boulders with eerie blue lights pulsating from them. They made a very loud wailing sound. All my attention was riveted right there . . . [The noise] was very loud and crashing, like whole mountains were moving . . . The blue was very deep. . . . and very blue, the most blue of blue . . . It was like drums beating so loud that you think they are your heartbeat. It was the Presence, whatever that means . . . The Presence was all around . . . It filled my heart and soul.[15]

This dream of the Presence gave Ruth peace. Astonishingly, after a second similar dream, Ruth called her daughter, with whom she had a fraught relationship, and found her daughter had also had a boulder dream. The two of them grew closer. A few nights later, Ruth had the dream again, but this time the boulders "had flattened into stepping stones and had moved to make sort of a path and were singing sweetly like the gentle wind. In the distance was a soft inviting clear golden light, it was the Presence calling me . . . It's calling me now and I want to go." Ruth died peacefully the next day, surrounded by her family. Her dreaming experience, and her death, deeply moved the hospice workers who attended her.

In the dream, Ruth's Presence is also a Place: a landscape that fills her heart and soul. Ruth is seeing the mystery that is the Presence within our world. This mystery gives her courage to approach her own death with surrender and serenity. She has experienced life "that transcends the grave." Such dreams, Patricia

Bulkley points out, heal the fear of the dying and help the living to face death without denial.

DREAMS AND THE CIRCLE OF LIFE

Some of our dreams do not only relate to our personal existence, but show us our place in the chain of generations. Ela, an artist and kohenet, shared a death-and-rebirth dream that suggested the connection between generations past and future.

> *Three white women, eyes closed, lie in a shallow grave, a square dug out of the grassy earth at Dunderry Park in County Meath. I see the middle woman—myself—sit up, awake and alive.*

In this dream, there are three women in a grave. However, the middle woman, who is also the dreamer, arises, alive. It is unclear whether the middle woman has died and come back to life, or whether a living woman has been lying in the grave with the two dead women.

This powerful dream image speaks for itself. Ela is connected to women in the earth—her ancestors from before her, and those yet to be born. The Talmud relates that the souls of the righteous dead and the souls of the unborn are stored in the same divine treasury.[16] Ela is dreaming a mythic dream where she is a living element in a long chain of lives that have existed and will continue to exist. She, too, will die—and perhaps has died before, if one considers the possibility of souls being reborn—but right now she is the living link, bringing the past into the present and the present into the future.

Dream researcher Jayne Gackenbach reports a dream of a Cree woman in Alberta in which the dreamer sat in a circle of trees and her deceased mother walked toward her, but disappeared just before reaching her.[17] Later in her life, after she became a parent, this same dreamer had another dream in which she became the mother in the dream, reaching for her daughter's hand within the circle of trees. The dreamer woke up to discover her daughter had just been rescued from a dangerous situation. The circle of trees had joined her and her daughter in loving presence, just as it had once joined her and her mother. We might even say the circle of trees is an image of the Tree of Life—or the web of being. When we are in that circle—"bound up in the bond of life" as the Jewish funeral liturgy says—we can touch one another across time, and even across life and death.

Death-and-rebirth dreams offer an initiatory experience. They signal change that may feel like (or even really be) the end of our present lives—literally or figuratively. Scholar of mythology and anthropology Michael Meade suggests that "every initiation causes a funeral and a birth: a mourning appropriate to death and a joyous celebration for the restoration of life."[15] Working with such dreams means opening to our feelings, even if they are overwhelming—and opening to the changes the dreams herald.

Like a sacred union dream, a death-and-rebirth dream is a gift, one that may come with intense feelings. Be gentle with yourself after one of these dreams. If the dream was scary, you can use prayer or meditation or a cup of hot tea to return to center. If you wish, you can use this prayer from the Talmud:

רִבּוֹנוֹ שֶׁל עוֹלָם אֲנִי שֶׁלָּךְ וַחֲלוֹמוֹתַי שֶׁלָּךְ:
חֲלוֹם חָלַמְתִּי וְאֵינִי יוֹדֵעַ מַה הוּא. אִם
טוֹבִים הֵם—חַזְּקֵם וְאַמְּצֵם כַּחֲלוֹמוֹתָיו
שֶׁל יוֹסֵף. וְאִם צְרִיכִים רְפוּאָה—רְפָאֵם
כְּמִרְיָם מִצָּרַעְתָּהּ. כֵּן הֲפוֹךְ כָּל חֲלוֹמוֹתַי עָלַי
לְטוֹבָה.

Source of Life, I am Yours and my dreams are Yours. I have dreamed a dream and I do not know what it means. If the dreams are good, strengthen them like the dreams of Joseph. And if the dreams are bad, heal them as You once healed

Miriam…Transform all of my dreams
for the good.[19]

As you remember the dream, see if you can find a moment
of change or rebirth. Feel into that moment. Consider
whether something like that is unfolding, or could unfold, in your waking life. Ask yourself how the dream is
advising you to navigate this shift in your world. Or, ask
a friend or wise confidante to reflect on the dream and
suggest what its message might be for you.

If your dream is comforting, that's a blessing. If your
dream is frightening, remember that it is not necessarily
a literal prophecy of things to come, nor does it mean
anything bad is going on inside you. It may simply be
alerting you to change, and the feelings that are coming
up around that change. If the dream is confusing, be
patient. It may be that more will become clear over time.

And if you or someone you love is facing the end
of life, know that dreams can offer hope and courage
around the transformations to come. A friend recently
wrote to tell me that her father has been dreaming of
his other daughter and his sister, both deceased, who
told him he should come with them. My friend received
the dreams as a premonition of her father's eventual
death, and found comfort in his visions of loved ones
who would welcome him. Dreams like this help us to
cope with our miraculous and fragile journeys on earth.

In a sense, every dream where we face death is a
death-and-rebirth dream, because we wake up at the
end. My experience is that sitting with these dreams
over time can eventually lead to moments of initiation,
renewal, and transformation. And when we come to the
end of our lives, these dreams can invite us into the
portal that takes us beyond everything we know.

Dreaming
the Circle

—

Guidance for
Dream Groups

In November 2017, Skye met with me to discuss her visionary dreams. During that meeting, Skye shared a dream she'd had that morning, and wondered why she'd had it on that particular day.

In the dream, she climbed to a university or temple on a large mountain, with thick fog everywhere. A circle of women was gathering together, yet Skye's attention was drawn beyond the circle, beyond the fog, toward mountain peaks she hadn't seen before. She decided to seek them out.

I find an overgrown trail leading through a small valley. I follow the trail as it slowly ascends the peak on the right side. As I emerge from a cloud of fog, I feel warmth radiating from the earth below. I come to a v-shaped intersection, and look up to see large mossy stone-carved stairs covered in vines and leaves, hardly visible as they blend into the mountainside. I wonder who built the trail, and when was the last time anyone had been up here to care for it.

Climbing the stairs, I carefully step in between the vines and rubble, as I notice a change in the landscape and the climate. The air becomes crisp and sweet. The steps are wet and the moss is cleared. I find my footing more easily than before. I'm able to look up ahead to see where I am going. I see above me a semicircle of five great guardian oak trees with intertwined branches, illuminated with the rising sun's golden rays. I am in awe of the beauty and take a moment to gratefully breathe in the new air. I notice a hint of a rainbow above the fog below me.

The trail curves to the left of the oak trees. I follow the path upwards and around the side of the

Epilogue: Dreaming the Circle

189

mountain and come upon a plateau below an-
other great mountain peak. In a clearing of bright
green grass, a circle of large gray stones like
Stonehenge glimmers and reflects the sun's light.

I walk toward the center and notice this area
has been cleared and maintained with care.
The oaks are behind the circle and I begin to
hear a high pitched singing-bowl sound. I look
up to see a ball of light above me that becomes
a column of light in the center of the stone circle.

When I heard Skye's dream, I cried, not only because of its beauty, but because it intersected with one of my own. You see, a few years before, I had visited Stonehenge. It was a gray and drizzly day, we had come on a tour bus (which is not a conducive context for spiritual encounter), my five-year-old daughter was wailing, and the experience wasn't at all transcendent. We weren't allowed to stand inside the stones or touch them. I went home grateful I'd seen the gray stones under the cloudy sky, but also deeply disappointed.

However, months later, I had a dream in which I visited Stonehenge again. There was no fence this time, and I went directly to the center of the circle of stones. At the center, I found a place where my voice echoed oddly. I invited the people around me to listen as I made humming sounds, playing with the resonance at the center of the circle. As I sang and hummed, I recognized the sound I was producing. It was exactly like playing a singing bowl.

When Skye told me her dream, I felt that we had been to the same sacred stone circle, and we had both heard the same resonant humming sound, the same music of the cosmos. I like to think that, in my dream, as I called people to listen to the singing-bowl sound, I called to Skye, and that Skye, on her pilgrimage to the mountain, heard me singing. We didn't know each other then, but we were both in a Place larger than ourselves. The kabbalists say that when we dream, we all travel to the Presence, and for Skye and me in that moment, it felt true.

All of us dreamers, we are all in that Place together, that underground temple where the stones sing, where the branches of the trees intertwine. That is the place where what connects us matters more than what divides us. That is the place we need to go in the real world, if we are to live well on this wondrous planet.

We need to keep this Place alive for ourselves, to listen for what it has to say. Living with our dreams as guides is an ancient practice of our ancestors, though it may or may not be the custom of our family or the society around us. When we begin to share the wisdom of our dreams, we not only start to see the world in a new light, we start to know one another in deeper, more vulnerable ways. That, too, is what we need now—to know one another not for what we can produce, but for what we feel, and what we love.

Many of my students, when we first begin to learn together about dreams, say that they can't recall their dreams or that they don't dream anything significant. Yet when they've set an intention to dream, when they've made themselves open to the idea that they do dream and that it matters, they begin to remember. And when they're part of a community that is eager to listen to their dreams, they begin to remember even more. Sharing dreams with one another becomes an act of love and trust. And sometimes, as Skye and I did, we dream together.

HOW TO CREATE AND GUIDE
A DREAM CIRCLE

A dream circle is a community whose members share and interpret their dreams—though I prefer the expression "reading" to "interpreting," as if one were ritually reading a sacred text. The circle should have a facilitator or leader to create a safe container for sharing, but the assumption is that everyone can bring their own wisdom to the dreams shared within the circle.

I began leading dream circles with Taya Mâ Shere, cofounder of the Kohenet Hebrew Priestess Institute, and still use much of the dream-reading ritual I learned from her, and which she adapted for Jewish dreamwork from the work of her teacher and collaborator LaKota OneHeart.[1] My current dream circle structure also incorporates elements of the dream interpretation methods of Dr. Catherine Shainberg and Robert Moss.[2] Below are the steps I use in my dream circle process. You can choose to adapt any of these to create your own dream community.

Remember, the Talmud says: "There were twenty-four dream interpreters in Jerusalem. Once I dreamed a dream and went to all of them; each one offered a different interpretation, and they all came true."[3] There are multiple truths in a dream. The goal of a dream circle is not to determine the one "right" meaning of a dream, but to open multiple pathways to wisdom and healing.

I. OPENING THE DREAM CIRCLE

Your dream circle could meet once a week, once a month, or even just one time. When the dream circle meets, you can begin with a song, poem, prayer, or the lighting of a candle. Introduce the participants to each other by name.

If you want to warm people up, particularly if the group is large or not everyone knows each other, put people in pairs or trios for five-to-eight minutes to share a single image from a dream they had and how it made them feel. (This way, if not everyone gets to share in the full circle, they at least get to share something of their own.) The other person in the pair or trio should silently witness the dream, rather than offering a dream reading.

II. IDENTIFYING THE DREAMER

Then, it's time to find out who wants to share a full dream with the whole group. In smaller dream circles, everyone can share a dream at every circle. This kind of dream circle creates a sense of deep closeness among the dreamers. In other, larger circles, only one or two people share a dream. This kind of circle can also be very powerful as one hears many perspectives on a single dream. My experience is that being a reader of someone else's dream (what Dr. Catherine Shainberg calls "a secondary dreamer") can be just as powerful and healing as sharing a dream of one's own.

I like to ask everyone to take a moment to discern if they have a dream to share that feels important to them and/or has medicine for the group. Then I ask how many people want to share. I try to make room for everyone, but if there are too many, I choose based on who replied first or who seems to have the most need to share. When necessary, you can also ask people to pull straws or slips of paper.

III. DREAM RITUAL

In the Talmud, when someone is disturbed by a dream, they can bring the dream to a "dream court"—a group of three people who ameliorate the dream (that is, improve the dream's impact). The dreamer says: "I have seen a good dream," and the court responds, "Good it is, and good may it be."[4] In my dream circle, we use something like this to begin a dream process: the dreamer says, "I have seen a good dream," and the group says, "Good it is, and good may it be." Or, we use a shorter version, where the group begins by telling the dreamer: "You have seen a good dream."

However, you could choose to do something else, like light a candle for each dream that is shared. Sometimes in my dream circles, we sing a song before each dream. The important thing is to honor the telling of each dream, and treat it as sacred.

IV. SHARING THE DREAM

The dreamer shares the dream. Sometimes, the person reads from a written record of the dream. (It's good if the rest of the group has a copy too; you can ask participants to email or print out the written dream.) Sometimes, the person tells the dream from memory. If it's a longish dream, or if the dream is not written down, the leader of the dream circle may ask the dreamer to repeat the dream twice so that everyone can remember the details.

It's best for the dreamer to share the dream in the present tense: for example, "I walk down the path and meet a large bear," not "I walked down the path and met a large bear." This helps the dream feel real in the moment. The recounting of the dream thus becomes an invocation, inviting all present to enter the dream as witnesses.

It's good for the dreamer to include as many details as they remember. The dreamer may also choose to include some very brief context, such as: "It was New Year's Day," or "I'd just had an argument with my spouse." But the dreamer should avoid interpreting their own dream (for example, "I think this dream is telling me to find a new job"). There will be time for that later, but at this point the goal is to describe the dream's events, sensations, and emotions.

If the dream feels intense or deeply significant to the dreamer, be sensitive. Still use the form that is suggested here, but move from stage to stage gently, making space for the dreamer's feelings. Be aware that people's dreams can bring up feelings for others as well. Hold the form of the circle carefully so the dreamer and community can feel safe. Don't allow advice giving or "caretaking" (for example, phrases like "everything will be okay," or "don't cry"). Make space for tears or laughter, but keep continuing with the process as described below, unless the dreamer asks to stop or pause.

Sometimes a dreamer wants to share a dream from a long time ago: a memorable nightmare, an important dream that affected them profoundly, or a dream that confused them. A dream that was dreamed years ago can still be very potent for the dreamer, and the dreamer can still benefit from the healing in the dream. I do invite people to share dreams from long ago if they wish. But in an ongoing dream circle, mostly the invitation is to share fresh dreams that are arising from within and speaking to the current moment.

V. CLARIFYING QUESTIONS

After the dreamer shares, the members of the circle may ask questions. These questions are meant to help the interpreters accurately perceive the dream, so that we can visualize the dream as clearly as possible. We engage this stage so we don't make mistakes like assuming a dream monster is scary when the dreamer thought it was cute, or thinking a dream landscape is ugly when the dreamer found it beautiful.

This is a delicate stage because the questions should stay close to the details of the dream itself, rather than venturing into interpretations or questions about the dreamer's past. They should focus attention on senses, feelings, and events, rather than abstractions or analysis. Examples of good questions are: "What color was the cat in the dream?" "How did it feel to discover the bridge across the lake?" "Do you remember anything about the person who was with you?" "Did anything happen between the party and the scene in the desert?" and "How did you feel about your mother in the dream?" However, at this stage of the process, some kinds of questions should be avoided, for example: "Did the character remind you of anything?" "What is your relationship with your mother like?" "Does the dream relate to any childhood trauma?" or "Do cats symbolize anything for you?" If the dreamer brings up these kinds of associations, that's fine, but the dream circle should not ask such questions as they put the dreamer in an analytical or therapeutic space, and may also violate the dreamer's privacy. I have seen Dr. Shainberg be very strict about this, to the point of interrupting the questioner rather than allow an invasive question.

In my experience, one shouldn't let the questioning phase go on for more than a few minutes, so that the dream's emotional energy doesn't dissipate. Unless the dream is unusually complicated, allow four to six questions and move on. The leader of the dream circle can also ask questions, and *should* if they think that others haven't clarified all the important details.

VI. DREAM-JOURNEYING

In my dream circles, after the questioning stage has concluded, I ask for a few moments of silence. During this silence, all the people in the circle (with the exception of the dreamer) recall the details of the dream and attempt to visualize or experience the dream as fully as possible. (During this time, the dreamer can meditate or pray for a good understanding of the dream.)

If thoughts, images, and feelings come to the participants during this time, they can weave those thoughts, images, and feelings into what they later say about the dream. They can also use the silence to focus their positive intention on the dreamer and ask that they receive what they need from the dream circle.

VII. READING THE DREAM

The leader of the circle now says, "The circle is open for dreams of this dream," or something else that indicates it is now time for the group to reflect on the dream. Each person shares their view of the dream and/or indicates what healing or wisdom might be in the dream. Each person begins their sharing by saying, "In my dream of this dream," a phrase I learned from Taya Mâ Shere.[5]

It is crucial, in this method, that each person who is opening the dream speak in the "I." That is, if there was a river in the dream, I might say: "The flowing of the river teaches me that everything changes," or "I feel called to fully immerse in the river of my life," or "I see the river as a portal to deeper consciousness," or "I love the feel of the water on my skin," or "The river invites me to immerse in the element of water." I would not say: "The river is telling you that you need to go with the flow," or "The river is asking you to let go of your attachment." This basic method of working with a dream has also been taught by Robert Moss (though in his dream circles, the phrase used at the beginning of a share is: "If it were my dream . . . ").[6]

Speaking in the first person prevents the interpreter from projecting onto the dreamer; as a result, the interpreter is less likely to use the dream to give advice to the dreamer (which is not the point of a dream circle). Using the first person also reminds everyone that each dream reader has a view of one facet of the dream—not its whole meaning. This method also allows the dream reader to stay in their senses and avoid overly abstracting or intellectualizing the dream. Further, this method reminds us that the dream holds healing and truth not only for the dreamer, but for everyone who hears the dream as well.

When sharing a dream, you can think about the dream structures you've learned about in this book. Where do you see dream portals, guardians, or healers? What obstacles or gifts can you find in the dream? Are there dream landscapes that feel like a powerful Place, or characters or entities that feel like a loving Presence? What is the message of these places and characters? If the dream is a nightmare, where are the demons in the dream? If the dream offers healing, where do you see healing in the dream? Is there a moment of union or rebirth? Does the dream offer any practical wisdom for waking life? Is the earth itself speaking in this dream?

You can offer an understanding of the entire dream, or of just one aspect. Both of these kinds of reflections can be helpful. I do find that if I read a dream, it's good to check if my way of understanding the dream fits with all the details of the dream. That's one way I test whether I am reading the dream successfully.[7]

You may want to ask each reader of the dream to say "I have spoken" when they are finished (or in Hebrew, *deebartee*). The group then responds: "I have heard" (or in Hebrew, *shamatee*). This practice, popularized in the Jewish Renewal[8] movement, ensures that everyone will know when someone is done speaking, and will witness that the person has spoken. (You can also have the dreamer do this when sharing the dream.)

I try to give everyone who wants to share a dream reading an opportunity to do so (and in small dream circles, often everyone does). If it is a large circle and many people want to share, it is okay to stop the sharing at some point; one doesn't want to overwhelm the dreamer or let the circle run too long. As the leader of a circle, I try to share last, unless few people are volunteering, in which case I add my dream opening somewhat earlier.

The Zohar says that we should only share dreams with a friend,[9] which essentially means that we should only share our dreams with people who have our best interests at heart. When you offer your reading, remember that you are looking for the healing in the dream. It's okay if you see a hard truth in the dream, but try to phrase your understanding of the dream in a way that emphasizes what's healing rather than what's difficult.

If someone who is reading a dream does not use the method—that is, they don't speak in the "I," and/or they begin giving advice to the dreamer as a "you" (e.g., "This dream means you should ..." or "This dream tells me that you experienced ...")— it can feel very awkward to interrupt. However, I generally do, and briefly ask the speaker to follow the established dream circle practices. The structure of the circle keeps people safe, lets everyone know what to expect, and ensures that no one will receive observations about their character or aggressive advice they didn't ask for. Just interrupt as gently and kindly as you can and reframe, and then invite the speaker to continue.

VIII. THE DREAMER SPEAKS

At the end of the process for each dream, I always invite a brief response from the dreamer. Sometimes the response is as simple as "thank you." Sometimes the dreamer will take the opportunity to share their own perspective on the dream, and/or offer gratitude for dream readings offered in the circle that have made an impact on them. Sometimes the dreamer will indicate a course of action that they plan to take in response to the dream. The group witnesses this response and thanks the dreamer for offering their dream.

IX. CLOSING THE DREAM

If you want, you can close each dream sharing with one of these brief prayers:

> "May this dream be a blessing for you and for all of us."
> "May the Presence continue to send you dreams of wisdom and healing."
> "(Name), we have witnessed your dream. It is a good dream, it is a good dream, it is a good dream."[10]

The process can then be repeated as time allows.

X. CLOSING THE CIRCLE

When the whole circle is complete, you can offer a song to close, or you can offer a collective "dream incubation" prayer where everyone asks for dream wisdom in the week or month to come. Here's a sample of such a prayer:

מְקוֹר חַיִּים תַּשְׁכִּיבֵנוּ לְשָׁלוֹם וְתַעֲמִידֵנוּ לְשָׁלוֹם וּתְהֵא
מִטָּתֵנוּ שְׁלֵמָה לְפָנֶיךָ: בָּרוּךְ אַתָּה נוֹתֵן חֲלוֹמוֹת.

Source of Life, help us to lie down in peace
and rise up in peace. May our sleep be whole
before You. Blessed are You, Giver of dreams.[11]

Or:

מְקוֹר חַיִּים—שְׁכִינָה קְדוֹשָׁה—פִּתְחִי לָנוּ פִּתְחֵי מַעֲלָה
וּפִתְחֵי מַטָּה פִּתְחֵי אֱמֶת פִּתְחֵי נְבוּאָה הַלַּיְלָה וְהַלֵּילוֹת
הַבָּאִים.

Source of Life, Sacred Presence, open up for
us the entrances up above and down below,
doors of truth and doors of prophecy, during
this night and the nights to come.[12]

Or combine them both!

At the end of the circle, it's good for the leader to be available
for a little bit in case anyone wants to share something privately
or process some feelings. Sometimes someone is too shy to share
a dream with a group but wants to share it with one person. And
sometimes what has been shared about the dream stirs up feelings for a dreamer, and the dreamer may want to talk about what
has come up for them.

DREAM *CHEVRUTA*/
HAVING A DREAM COMPANION

If you don't have the resources for a dream circle, or want ad-
ditional time for sharing dreams, you can still benefit from the
process described above if you have another person who works
on dreams with you. In my community, we call this a dream

chevruta. (A *chevruta* is an ancient Hebrew/Aramaic term for a study partner or friend.) If there is someone else in your life who is interested in dream practice, you can support one another by sharing dreams on a daily, weekly, or even monthly basis.

Your process can be as simple as sharing your dreams and offering thoughts on what the healing and/or message of the dream might be. Or you can go through the above ten steps together.

Some people like to have a dreamworker who meets with them in a dedicated way and serves as a counselor, working through dreams that feel significant. Your dreamworker might help you explore feelings that arise, or suggest images or truths within the dream that you may want to integrate into your waking life.

However you decide to work with your dreams, having someone to share dreams with will help you to remember your dreams and bring their wisdom and healing into your world.

A NOTE ON RECORDING ONE'S DREAMS

In order to remember, work with, and share our dreams with others, it's essential to keep track of them, whether on paper or in a voice recording. This requires diligent practice. Often, if we wait to record a dream, we forget important details or forget the dream entirely. The important thing, even if we don't remember the whole dream, is to record as much as we can.

When you write down a dream, try to get the basic narrative first, so you don't forget it. Then, go back and fill in details: what you remember about characters, places, emotions, motivations, etc. If you encountered a song or an artwork, it's helpful to try to replicate it—to sing or to draw it. Try to make the dream report as alive and sensual as the dream actually felt. Be sure to record how you felt during the dream: otherwise, you may look over the images later and not be sure what the dream's impact was at the time you dreamed it.

Sometimes, when we record a dream, we find ourselves filling in details we don't actually remember in order to make the dream feel coherent. Try, to the best of your ability, to stick to what you really do remember. If the dream is incomplete or doesn't make sense, that's okay. Just tell it the way you remember it.

Dream recall can be difficult; our brain chemistry actually attempts to erase our dreams upon awakening.[13] So we have to catch the dream right away. Some people need to write their dreams down before they turn the lights on or before they get up from bed to preserve all the details. Some of us find we remember best when we aren't woken up by an alarm; for others, it's the opposite. Figure out what kind of dreamer you are and make your recording plan based on what you need.

I have periods of time where I remember very few dreams and periods where I remember many. In my experience, the keys to remembering dreams are:

1) Don't get frustrated or give up if you don't remember at first; just try again with the next dream if you forget.
2) Have a chosen method for recording the dream (pen and paper, texting, making a voice note, etc.).
3) Have a supportive context to share the dream, at least some of the time. If you know someone is waiting to hear your dream, it may help you remember.
4) Always, or almost always, try to record a remembered dream. Regular practice helps you remember more dreams.

Don't throw records of old dreams away. I now have dream records going back many years. It is a gift to be able to read over my dreams, notice new things about them, and observe larger patterns. Sometimes a dream I didn't understand becomes clear years later. A dream diary can not only help to shape our days, but can help us powerfully reflect on our lives.

RETURN TO THE UNDERGROUND TEMPLE

I want to end as I began: with a dream of the underground temple.

I am in a miles-high castle on a mountain. The castle is so immense that a whole society lives in it, a society that I sense is rules-based, corrupt, and uncaring about its citizens. An elder woman instructs me that I must go to the lowest level of the castle. There is an elevator to get there, but it is not a normal elevator. It is a round disk of stone. This elevator has no pulley; the disk just falls down the shaft. I get into the elevator with a few other women and then we are in free fall, for long moments down the shaft, through volcanic rock to the heart of the mountain. It is terrifying; I am certain we will die. The disk lands and we are safe, but I am scared.

Later, I have to go back up in the elevator. I am afraid that if I don't get there before the elevator leaves, I'll be lost in the dark of the mountain. But I do make it in time, and the elevator ascends. Once again I have an awful feeling, but I get out safely at the top of the castle.

Now the elder woman has another quest for me: I have to go down and spy out an approaching army that threatens the people of the castle. She asks me to go in the elevator again, but I am so afraid that I say I would rather climb the miles of stairs that thread through the mountain's volcanic rock. The elder woman says it

will take two weeks of hiking through under-
ground mountain passages to get to the bottom.
I say I will do it.

On my journey, there are bridges over flowing
lava, strange landforms, and passages through
stone. When I finally come out at the bottom,
I realize the landscape looks just like the hilly
terrain of my childhood home, except that the
hill is covered in rivers and smooth, slippery
volcanic rock.

Suddenly, I see women from my spiritual com-
munity. They're riding the rivers and the slides
of volcanic rock and having a great time, as if
the landscape is a roller coaster. They're slid-
ing down one hill as I am climbing up another,
and we are cheering each other on. They're yell-
ing at me: "You can do it, you can make it to the
top, and when you do, you're going to love it."

This dream is a journey dream, a portal dream, a nightmare, and a healing dream all at once. I begin in a castle inhabited by a callous and rigid society (maybe reminiscent of the society I inhabit in waking life). When a guide directs me to go to the bottom of the mountain, I have to take an elevator that is not an elevator but a stone disk that falls through empty space. The fall is terrifying, and after my first trip, I race back up because I am afraid: afraid of being left behind, of being lost and forgotten, of losing my connection to the world above.

The second time I am sent down the mountain, I go on my own terms: I take a weeks-long journey through wondrous volcanic caves. When I finally come to the bottom, I am at my childhood home. I have found the Place. There, instead of my family's hilly, grassy lawn, are rivers flowing over volcanic rock—the very same image I described in the dream at the beginning of this book. This landscape of flowing water and fire and earth—of elemental forces shaping the planet—is my vision of the underground temple. It is unique to me, the way your image, in your own dreams, is unique to you.

When I arrive, I discover the bottom of the mountain isn't a scary place after all. My spiritual community is there, having a magnificent time sliding on the water and stone. They are the Presence that welcomes me. As I climb to the top of a hill, they cheer me on, telling me I am going to love what I find at the end of the journey. I was so scared to get here, and all I ever had to do was let go and fall into the dream, into the unconscious connection we have to the elements in our molecules, to the life of our world, to the Presence that fills and surrounds all things. Letting go into that Place is one of the gifts of being alive.

The Place, as we find it in dreams, is never stagnant. It is always unfolding and changing, unclogging channels, awakening knowledge, and introducing new paradigms. That is why the Place, the Presence, heals. It bursts through our rigid thought patterns. It moves us beyond philosophy, religion, logic, and sacred text to our own visceral knowing, our experience of the life force. It is an Undertorah, a revelatory undercurrent beneath the daily hum of our being.

I am so grateful to the dreamers who have told me their dreams, and shared stories of transformation and healing. I bless all of us dreamers who make these wild journeys every night. I offer deepest gratitude to the dreamers of my home tradition, and the dreaming ancestors of all cultures, for leaving us clues to the mysterious wisdom we encounter in the dark. And finally, I reverently bow to the underground temple and its mysteries. May the Presence guide each of us where we need to go.

Endnotes

INTRODUCTION

1. Zohar I, 200a.

2. Rodger Kamenetz, *The History of Last Night's Dream: Discovering the Hidden Path to the Soul* (New York: HarperOne, 2007), 98–107.

3. Leonard Shlain, *The Alphabet Versus the Goddess: The Conflict Between Word and Image* (New York: Penguin Compass, 1999).

4. Natalie Weaver, "In Dreams," *Feminism and Religion*, October 2, 2019, https://feminisman-dreligion.com/2019/10/02/in-dreams-by-natalie-weaver/.

5. Zohar I, 149a.

6. Babylonian Talmud, Berakhot 55b.

7. Muriel Rukeyser, "Akiba," in *The Collected Poems of Muriel Rukeyser*, eds. Janet E. Kaufman and Anne F. Herzog (Pittsburgh: University of Pittsburgh Press, 2005), 454.

CHAPTER 1: GROUNDING IN OUR DREAMS

1. Patricia Bulkley, "Invitation at the Threshold: Pre-Death Spiritual Experiences," in *Among All These Dreamers: Essays on Dreaming and Modern Society*, ed. Kelly Bulkeley (Albany, NY: State University of New York Press, 1996), 163–164.

2. *Castle in the Sky*, written and directed by Hayao Miyazaki (Tokyo: Studio Ghibli, 2003).

3. Ninad Gujar, Steven Andrew McDonald, Masaki Nishida, and Matthew P. Walker, "A Role for REM Sleep in Recalibrating the Sensitivity of the Human Brain to Specific Emotions," *Cerebral Cortex* 21 (January 2011).

4. Matthew Wilson, "Animals Have Complex Dreams, MIT Researcher Proves," *MIT News,* January 24, 2001, http://news.mit.edu/2001/dreaming.

5. Erik Hoel, "The Overfitted Brain: Dreams Evolved to Assist Generalization," *Patterns* 2, no. 5 (May

2021), https://doi.org/10.1016/j.
patter.2021.100244.

6. Kate Kellaway, "When We Dream,
We Have the Perfect Chemical Canvas
for Intense Visions," *The Guardian*,
April 14, 2019, https://www.theguard-
ian.com/science/2019/apr/14/
dreams-perfect-canvas-intense-vi-
sions-alice-robb-interview.

7. "Anishinabe Dreams," *Native
American Netroots*, September 25,
2010, http://nativeamericannetroots.
net/diary/691.

8. Tika Yupanqui (Tracy Marks),
"The Iroquois Dream Experience and
Spirituality, Part One," WebWinds,
1998, http://www.webwinds.com/
yupanqui/iroquoisdreams.htm.

9. Fidel Moreno (Native shaman),
private conversation with author,
2016; Jean-Guy A. Goulet, "Dreams
and Visions in Indigenous Lifeworlds:
An Experiential Approach," *Canadian
Journal of Native Studies* 13, no. 2
(1993): 177, http://www3.brandonu.
ca/cjns/13.2/goulet.pdf.

10. Zohar I, 200a.

11. E. E. Cummings, "maggie
and milly and molly and may,"
in *Complete Poems: 1904–1962*, by
E. E. Cummings, ed. George J. Firmage,
rev. ed. (New York: Liveright
Publishing Corporation, 2016), 723.

12. Hayyim Vital, "Book of Visions," in
*Jewish Mystical Autobiographies: Book
of Visions and Book of Secrets*, trans.
and ed. Morris M. Faierstein (Mahwah,
NJ: Paulist Press, 1999), 137–138.
Translation adjusted.

13. Eli Yassif, *The Legend of Safed: Life
and Fantasy in the City of Kabbalah*,
trans. Haim Watzman (Detroit: Wayne
State University Press, 2019), 161–
162. The phrase "as beautiful as the
sun" is Vital's. The latter description
("a wondrous yard . . .") comes from
Yassif's retelling of Vital's dream.

14. Zohar I, 70b.

15. Zalman Schachter-Shalomi, "The
Spirituality of the Future: Toward a
New and Kerygmatic Credo," The
Shalom Center, May 9, 2008, https://
theshalomcenter.org/node/1395;
Leah Novick, "Shekhinah Theology
of the Future," *Delumin/a*, March 15,
2015, http://delumina.net/blog/tag/
Leah+Novick.

16. Zohar Hadash, quoted in David
Seidenberg, *Kabbalah and Ecology:
God's Image in the More-Than-
Human World* (Cambridge: Cambridge
University Press, 2016), 211.

17. David Abram, *The Spell of the
Sensuous: Perception and Language in
a More-Than-Human World* (New York:
Vintage Books, 1997).

18. Stephan Harding, *Animate Earth: Science, Intuition and Gaia* (White River Junction, VT: Chelsea Green Publishing Company, 2006), 14.

19. Catherine Shainberg, quoted in "We Are Always Dreaming," interview by Tami Simon, *Insights at the Edge,* Sounds True, January 21, 2014, https://www.resources.soundstrue.com/podcast/we-are-always-dreaming/.

20. David Abram, *Becoming Animal: An Earthly Cosmology* (New York: Vintage Books, 2011), 4.

21. Zohar I, 149a.

22. Michael Lennox, *Dream Sight: A Dictionary and Guide for Interpreting Any Dream* (Woodbury, MN: Llewellyn Publications, 2011), 30.

23. C. G. Jung, "The Meaning of Psychology for Modern Man" (1933), in *Civilization in Transition: The Collected Works of C. G. Jung,* Vol. 10, ed. and trans. Gerhard Adler and R. F. C. Hull (Princeton, NJ: Princeton University Press, 1970), 323.

24. Stephen Aizenstat, *Dream Tending: Awakening to the Healing Power of Dreams* (New Orleans: Spring Journal, Inc., 2011), 264.

25. Aizenstat, *Dream Tending,* 149–150.

26. Rodger Kamenetz, "The Poetic Imagination and the Natural Dream," Natural Dreamwork, April 9, 2021, https://www.thenaturaldream.com/dream-poetry/.

27. The Kohenet Hebrew Priestess Institute, founded by Jill Hammer and Taya Mâ Shere, is a training program in earth-based, embodied, feminist Jewish spiritual leadership. A graduate of the program is called a "kohenet," a Hebrew word for priestess. Dreamwork is an important practice for the Kohenet community, and a number of the dreamers who offered their dreams for this book are ordinees of the Kohenet Hebrew Priestess Institute. The Kohenet Hebrew Priestess Institute's dream practice is described in: Jill Hammer and Taya Shere, *The Hebrew Priestess: Ancient and New Visions of Jewish Women's Spiritual Leadership* (Teaneck, NJ: Ben Yehuda Press, 2015), and is also referenced in the Epilogue.

28. Babylonian Talmud, Berakhot 55b.

29. Jill Hammer, *Return to the Place: The Magic, Meditation, and Mystery of Sefer Yetzirah* (Teaneck, NJ: Ben Yehuda Press, 2020), 192.

30. Midrash Tanhuma, Pekudei 3.

31. Meredith Sabini, "Dreaming for Our Survival," *Depth Insights,* Fall 2013, http://www.depthinsights.com/Depth-Insights-scholarly-

ezine/e-zine-issue-5-fall-2013/
dreaming-for-our-survival-by-mere-
dith-sabini/.

CHAPTER 2:
DREAMING THE
JOURNEY

1. Babylonian Talmud, Niddah 30b.
Literally, "A person can sleep here and
dream of Spain."

2. Hayyim Vital, "Book of Visions," in
*Jewish Mystical Autobiographies: Book
of Visions and Book of Secrets*, trans.
and ed. Morris M. Faierstein (Mahwah,
NJ: Paulist Press, 1999), 138–140.

3. Rodger Kamenetz understands
dream wandering as a search for
something deeper. Rodger Kamenetz,
*The History of Last Night's Dream:
Discovering the Hidden Path to the Soul*
(New York: HarperOne, 2007), 3–14.

4. Environmental Protection Agency
(EPA), *EPA's 2008 Report on the
Environment* (Washington, DC:
National Center for Environmental
Assessment, 2008), Chapter 2, 73,
https://cfpub.epa.gov/roe/documents/
EPAROE_final_2008.pdf.

5. Mary Jo Heyen, *Dreaming into the
Mystery: Exploring the Dreams and
Visions of the Dying* (Davey Press,
2020), 45.

CHAPTER 3:
ELEMENTAL PORTALS
TO THE PRESENCE

1. David Abram, *The Spell of the
Sensuous: Perception and Language in
a More-Than-Human World* (New York:
Vintage Books, 1997), 163.

2. Sharon Blackie, interview, The Shift
Network's Dreamwork Summit (online
conference), October 30, 2019.

3. Stephan Harding, *Animate Earth:
Science, Intuition and Gaia* (White
River Junction, VT: Chelsea Green
Publishing Company, 2006), 19.

4. Robert Moss, interview by Rodger
Kamenetz, The Shift Network's
Dreamwork Summit (online confer-
ence), October 29, 2019.

5. Jill Hammer, *Return to the Place:
The Magic, Meditation, and Mystery
of Sefer Yetzirah* (Teaneck, NJ: Ben
Yehuda Press, 2020), 101.

6. Otzar haMidrashim, Masechet Gan
Eden 4. The Masechet Gan Eden is a
medieval work that describes heaven
and hell in Jewish legend.

7. Brynn Myers, *The Echoed Life of
Jorja Graham*, 2nd ed. (Florida: Indigo
Ink Publications, 2021), 57.

8. "Havamal" (a collection of Old
Norse poems from the Viking Age),
stanza 138. Carolyne Larrington,

trans., *The Poetic Edda* (Oxford: Oxford University Press, 1996), 34.

9. Neil Gaiman, *The Ocean at the End of the Lane* (New York: William Morrow, 2016), 141.

10. Marie Fernandes, "The River as Metaphor," *Andrean Research Journal* 6 (2016–2017), https://standrewscollege.ac.in/wp-content/uploads/2018/06/The-River-as-Metaphor.pdf.

11. Anthony Shafton, *Dream-Singers: The African American Way with Dreams* (Hoboken, NJ: John Wiley and Sons, 2002), 154.

12. This insight comes from dream-worker Rodger Kamenetz—we can feel into the dream and go where it wants us to go, even if that is frightening.

13. Enuma Elish (a Babylonian creation myth). Leonard W. King, *Enuma Elish: The Seven Tablets of Creation; The Babylonian and Assyrian Legends Concerning the Creation of the World and Mankind*, rev. ed. (1902; repr., New York: Cosimo Classics, 2010).

14. Genesis 1:2.

15. Babylonian Talmud, Sukkah 53b.

16. Zohar III, 166b.

17. Ray Bradbury, *Something Wicked This Way Comes* (New York: Simon & Schuster, 1997), 8.

18. Toni Morrison, *Song of Solomon* (New York: Vintage International, 2004), 337.

19. Exodus 3:2–5.

20. Exodus 13:21; Leviticus 9:10.

21. Zohar II, 83b.

22. See Howard Schwartz, *Tree of Souls: The Mythology of Judaism* (Oxford: Oxford University Press, 2007), 122–123.

23. Exodus 3:5.

24. Babylonian Talmud, Berakhot 55b.

25. Simon Makin, "Deep Sleep Gives Your Brain a Deep Clean," *Scientific American*, November 1, 2019, https://scientificamerican.com/article/deep-sleep-gives-your-brain-a-deep-clean1/.

26. Arthur Rimbaud, *A Season in Hell and the Drunken Boat/Une Saison en Enfer et Le Bateau Ivre*, trans. Louise Varèse (New York: New Directions, 1961), 86.

27. Likutei Tefillot 11:224.

CHAPTER 4: GUARDIANS OF THE DREAM TEMPLE

1. David Abram, *The Spell of the Sensuous: Perception and Language in a More-Than-Human World* (New York: Vintage Books, 1997), 56.

2. Avivah Gottlieb Zornberg, *Moses: A Human Life* (New Haven, CT: Yale University Press, 2016), 58.

3. Genesis 28:17.

4. Hirsh Loeb Gordon, *The Maggid of Caro: The Mystic Life of the Eminent Codifier Joseph Caro as Revealed in His Secret Diary* (1949; repr., Whitefish, MT: Literary Licensing, 2013).

5. Kat Duff, *The Secret Life of Sleep* (London: Oneworld, 2014), 152.

6. Gnomes for earth, undines for water, sylphs for air, and salamanders for fire. For example, see *The Hermetic and Alchemical Writings of Paracelsus*, ed. Arthur Edward Waite (Eastford, CT: Martino Fine Books, 2009); Edmund Siderius, "Knowledge in Nature, Knowledge of Nature: Paracelsus and the Elementals," The Starry Messenger, March 8, 2011, https://edmundside-rius.wordpress.com/2011/03/08/knowledge-in-nature-knowledge-of-nature-paracelsus-and-the-elementals/.

7. Robert Moss, interview by Rodger Kamenetz, The Shift Network's Dreamwork Summit (online conference), October 29, 2019.

8. Likutei Moharan 2, 63.

9. Zohar II, 20a.

10. Babylonian Talmud, Avodah Zarah 3b.

11. Ursula K. Le Guin, *A Wizard of Earthsea* (Boston: Houghton Mifflin, 1968), 92.

12. Catherine Shainberg refers to dreams that diagnose blockages and attempt to remove them as "clearing dreams"—that is, they "clear" an obstacle.

13. Babylonian Talmud, Berakhot 55b.

CHAPTER 5: HEALING IN OUR DREAMS

1. Mary Jo Heyen, interview by Rodger Kamenetz, The Shift Network's Dreamwork Summit (online conference), November 1, 2019.

2. Jonathan Sharp, *Divining Your Dreams: How the Ancient Mystical Tradition of the Kabbalah Can Help You Interpret 1,000 Dream Images* (New York: Atria Books, 2002), 2. Translation adjusted.

3. Tika Yupanqui (Tracy Marks), "The Iroquois Dream Experience and Spirituality, Part One," WebWinds, 1988, http://www.webwinds.com/yupanqui/iroquoisdreams.htm.

4. Likutei Moharan 1, 5:1.

5. Lian Hearn, *Emperor of the Eight Islands: The Tale of Shikanoko, Book I* (New York: Farrar, Strauss, and Giroux, 2016), 184.

6. Nam-lin Hur, *Prayer and Play in Late Tokugawa Japan: Asakusa Sensōji and Edo Society* (Cambridge, MA: Harvard University Press, 2000), 84.

7. Shohama Wiener, "Rosh Hashanah 2009/5770: A Ladder to Heaven," Temple Beth-El of City Island, August 31, 2009, https://your-shulbythesea.org/2009/08/31/rosh-hashanah-20095770/.

CHAPTER 6:
ANCESTRAL HEALING
IN OUR DREAMS

1. David Abram, *The Spell of the Sensuous: Perception and Language in a More-Than-Human World* (New York: Vintage Books, 1997), 16.

2. Rivka Schiller, "'Psychic Dreams,' Witches, Curses, and Other Family Secrets," Rivka's Yiddish, June 25, 2017, http://www.rivkasyiddish.com/blog/psychic-dreams-witches-curses-and-other-family-secrets.

3. Rosemary Lévy Zumwalt, "Las Buenas Mujeres: The Keepers of Sephardic Health and Home," *Jewish Folklore and Etymology Review* 15, no. 2 (1993): 110.

4. See Jill Hammer and Taya Shere, *The Hebrew Priestess: Ancient and New Visions of Contemporary Jewish Women's Spiritual Leadership* (Teaneck, NJ: Ben Yehuda Press, 2015), 179.

5. Glückel, *The Life of Glückel of Hameln: A Memoir*, trans. and ed. Beth-Zion Abrahams (Philadelphia: Jewish Publication Society, 2012), 20, 97.

6. Tirzah Firestone, *Wounds into Wisdom: Healing Intergenerational Jewish Trauma* (Rhinebeck, NY: Monkfish, 2019), 1–2. Used with permission of the author.

7. Firestone, 2.

8. Susan Sered, *Women as Ritual Experts: The Religious Lives of Elderly Jewish Women in Jerusalem* (Oxford: Oxford University Press, 1992).

9. Hayyim Vital, "Book of Visions," in *Jewish Mystical Autobiographies: Book of Visions and Book of Secrets*, trans. and ed. Morris M. Faierstein (Mahwah, NJ: Paulist Press, 1999), 117. Translation adjusted.

10. Marion Wallace, "'Making Tradition': Healing, History and Ethnic Identity among Otjiherero-Speakers in Namibia, c. 1850–1950," *Journal of Southern African Studies* 29, no. 2 (June 2003): 355, https://doi.org/10.1080/03057070306212.

11. Hill Gates, "Money for the Gods," *Modern China* 13, no. 3 (July 1987): 259–277.

12. E. W. G. Masterman, "Jewish Customs of Birth, Marriage, and Death," *The Biblical World* 22, no. 4 (1903): 248–257. Also note the empty-chair work in psychodramatic settings and in bibliodrama. See Peter Pitzele, *Scripture Windows: Toward a Practice of Bibliodrama* (Los Angeles: Torah Aura Productions, 1998), 40.

13. This prayer is based on a Yiddish women's prayer for making soul candles, recorded in English in Chava Weissler, *Voices of the Matriarchs: Listening to the Prayers of Early Modern Jewish Women* (Boston: Beacon Press, 1998), 132–134. Kohenet and Yiddishist Annabel Cohen translated my revised prayer into Yiddish for this book. According to Eastern European Jewish custom, soul candles are made prior to Yom Kippur as a memorial to the dead, inviting them to pray for the living.

CHAPTER 7: DREAM-HEALING OUR WORLD

1. LaChelle Schilling, "Desierto Divino: Messages from the Earth," *Feminism and Religion*, February 17, 2017, https://feminismandreligion.com/2017/02/17/desierto-divino-messages-from-the-earth-by-lachelle-schilling/.

2. Wangari Maathai, "Nobel Lecture," The Nobel Prize, December 10, 2004, https://nobelprize.org/prizes/peace/2004/maathai/26050-wangari-maathai-nobel-lecture-2004/.

3. Sally Gillespie, "Climate Change and Psyche: Mapping Myths, Dreams and Conversations in the Era of Global Warming" (PhD diss., Western Sydney University, 2014), 4, http://researchdirect.uws.edu.au/islandora/object/uws%3A32281/datastream/PDF/view.

4. Zohar II, 142b.

5. Sha'arei Kedushah, Part 1, 3:6.

6. James Hillman, *The Dream and the Underworld* (New York: Harper and Row, 1979), 150.

7. Grandmother Flordemayo, "The Threads of Dreaming," interview by Kezia Vida, The Shift Network's Dreamwork Summit (online conference), November 1, 2019.

8. Thomas A. M. Pugh, Mats Lindeskog, Benjamin Smith, Benjamin Poulter, Almut Arneth, Vanessa Haverd, and Leonardo Calle, "Role of Forest Regrowth in Global Carbon Sink Dynamics," *Proceedings of the National Academy of Sciences of the United States of America* 116, no. 10 (2019): 4382–4387, https://doi.org/10.1073/pnas.1810512116; Sarah Gibbens, "Scientists Are Trying to Save Coral Reefs. Here's What's Working," *National Geographic*, June 4, 2020, https://national-geographic.com/science/article/scientists-work-to-save-coral-reefs-climate-change-marine-parks; Jessica A. Rubin and J. H. Görres, "Potential for Mycorrhizae-Assisted Phytoremediation of Phosphorus for Improved Water Quality," *International Journal of Environmental Research and Public Health* 18, no. 1 (January 2021), https://doi.org/10.3390/ijerph18010007.

9. Pirkei Avot 2:16.

CHAPTER 8: FACING OUR NIGHTMARES

1. John (Bear) Tate, interview, The Shift Network's Dreamwork Summit (online conference), October 31, 2019.

2. Babylonian Talmud, Berakhot 6a.

3. Babylonian Talmud, Chagigah 16a.

4. Zohar I, 200a.

5. Babylonian Talmud, Berakhot 6a.

6. Bette Ehlert, "Healing Crimes: Dreaming Up the Solution to the Criminal Justice Mess," in *Among All These Dreamers: Essays on Dreaming and Modern Society*, ed. Kelly Bulkeley (Albany, NY: State University of New York Press, 1996), 210–211.

7. Visualizing two opposing dream images to see what arises is a method I learned from Rodger Kamenetz, author of *The History of Last Night's Dream*.

8. From the traditional Jewish bedtime prayer, which can be located in a Jewish prayerbook, usually at the end of the evening service. The transliteration is: *Barukh atah Adonai Eloheinu melekh ha'olam hamapeel chevlei sheynah al eynay utenumah al afapay. Veehee ratzon meelifanekha Adonai Elohai ve'elohey avotai ve'eemotai shetash-keeveyni leshalom veta'amideynee leshalom ve'al tevahalooni rayoni vachalomot ra'eem vehirhurim ra'eem utehey meetatee shleymah lifanekha ve'ha'eyr eynay pen ishan hamavet ki atah hame'ir le'eeshon bat ayin. Barukh atah adonai hame'eer la'olam koolo beekhvodo.*

9. The transliteration of the feminine version is: *Berukhah at Shekhinah Eloheinu ruach ha'olam hamapeelah chevlei sheynah al eynay utenumah al afapay. Veehee ratzon meelifanayeekh*

*Shekhinah elohai ve'elohey avotai
ve'eemotai shetashkeeveeni leshalom veta'amideenee leshalom ve'al
tevahalooni rayoni vachalomot ra'eem
vehirhurim ra'eem utehey meetatee
shleymah lifanayikh ve'ha'eeree eynay
pen ishan hamavet ki at hame'irah
le'eeshon bat ayin. Berukhah at
Shekhinah hame'eerah la'olam koolo
beekhvodah.*

10. Samuel G. Armistead and Joseph
H. Silverman, "A Judeo-Spanish
Prayer," *La Corónica* 19, no. 1
(1990–1991): 22–31. Transliterated for
spoken Ladino by Dr. Devin Naar.

CHAPTER 9:
DREAMING THE
SACRED UNION

1. Zohar II, 133b.

2. These words are from the poem
"Lecha Dodi" (originally written
by Shlomo haLevi Alkabetz in the
sixteenth century), recited during the
traditional Jewish Friday night liturgy.

3. Zohar II, 63b.

4. Rodger Kamenetz, "The Sacred
Encounter in Our Dreams," Natural
Dreamwork and the Sacred Encounter
(class for The Shift Network, December
12, 2019, https://theshiftnetwork.com/
course/NaturalDreamwork).

5. David Abram, *Becoming Animal: An
Earthly Cosmology* (New York: Vintage
Books, 2011), 10.

6. This was shared with me by Kohenet
Renee Finkelstein. See Prateek
Pathak, "Why Lord Krishna Is Known
as 'Banke Bihari,'" *The Speaking
Tree*, March 23, 2015, https://www.
speakingtree.in/allslides/why-lord-
krishna-is-known-as-banke-bihari.

7. Diane Wolkstein and Samuel
Noah Kramer, *Inanna, Queen of
Heaven and Earth: Her Stories and
Hymns from Sumer* (San Francisco:
HarperPerennial, 1983), 123; Kim
McCone, *Pagan Past and Christian
Present in Early Irish Literature*
(Maynooth, Ireland: Maynooth
Monographs, 1990), 110; F. J. Byrne,
Irish Kings and High-Kings (London:
Batsford, 1973), 17; D. A. Binchy,
"The Fair of Tailtiu and the Feast of
Tara," *Ériu* 18 (1958): 134–5; Beate
Pongratz-Leisten, "Sacred Marriages
and the Transfer of Divine Knowledge:
Alliances between the Gods and the
King in Ancient Mesopotamia," in
*Sacred Marriages: The Divine-Human
Sexual Metaphor from Sumer to Early
Christianity*, eds. Martti Nissinen
and Risto Uro (Winona Lake, IN:
Eisenbrauns, 2008), 43–73.

8. Philip Ravenhill, *Dreams and Reverie:
Images of Otherworld Mates Among
the Baule, West Africa* (Washington,
DC: Smithsonian Institution Press,
1996), 2; Andrei A. Znamenski, ed.,

Shamanism: Critical Concepts in Sociology (London and New York: RoutledgeCurzon, 2004), 128.

9. Dare Sohei, "Musings from a Transformed Being," Think Movement, September 6, 2020, https://thinkmovement.net/2020/09/06/musings-from-a-transformed-being/.

10. This version of the myth was shared with me by Kohenet Renee Finkelstein. See also Wendy Doniger, "Kali," *Encyclopedia Britannica*, updated May 5, 2015, https://www.britannica.com/topic/Kali#ref942491.

11. Gerhard Dorn, quoted in C. G. Jung, *Mysterium Coniunctionis: The Collected Works of C. G. Jung*, Vol. 14, ed. and trans. Gerhard Adler and R. F. C. Hull (Princeton, NJ: Princeton University Press, 1977), 41.

12.
לְשֵׁם יִחוּד קוּדְשָׁא בְּרִיךְ הוּא וּשְׁכִינְתֵיה.
L'shem yichud kudsha brich hu ush'khintei.

CHAPTER 10:
DEATH AND REBIRTH
IN DREAMS

1. Patricia Monaghan, "Harvest Evening," in *Grace of Ancient Land* (New Orleans: Voices from the American Land, 2011), http://www.voicesfromtheamericanland.org/html/monaghan.html.

2. Jill Hammer, *Return to the Place: The Magic, Meditation, and Mystery of Sefer Yetzirah* (Teaneck, NJ: Ben Yehuda Press, 2020), 37.

3. C. G. Jung, *The Archetypes and the Collective Unconscious: The Collected Works of C. G. Jung*, Vol. 9 (Part I), ed. and trans. Gerhard Adler and R. F. C. Hull (Princeton, NJ: Princeton University Press, 1968), 117.

4. Babylonian Talmud, Ta'anit 2a.

5. Zohar III, 162b.

6. Karen Jaenke, "Dreaming with the Ancestors," *ReVision* 28, no. 4 (Spring 2006): 30.

7. Ezekiel 37:4.

8. Babylonian Talmud, Ta'anit 23a.

9. The story is found in the "Homeric Hymn to Aphrodite."

10. Rozie Apps, "Using Fungi to Clean Up Pollutants," *Permaculture Magazine*, February 5, 2015, https://www.permaculture.co.uk/readers-solutions/using-fungi-clean-pollutants.

11. Institut de Recherche pour le Développement (IRD), "Mangroves: A Filter for Heavy Metals," *ScienceDaily*, July 24, 2012, https://www.sciencedaily.com/releases/2012/07/120724104304.htm.

12. Manfred Dworschak, "Europe Gone Wild: Back to Nature on the Continent," trans. Christopher Sultan, *Spiegel Online*, October 24, 2013, https://www.spiegel.de/international/europe/rewilding-movement-seeks-to-return-areas-of-europe-to-wilderness-a-929573.html.

13. For example, in his book *The Healing Wisdom of Africa,* Malidoma Patrice Somé describes the grieving practices of the Dagara people by saying that the earth will absorb the grief. (See Malidoma Patrice Somé, *The Healing Wisdom of Africa: Finding Life Purpose through Nature, Ritual, and Community* [New York: TarcherPerigee, 1999], 55.) The Jewish tradition understands the ritual bath (often a body of naturally gathered water) as a spiritual cleansing agent, and Jewish tradition allows for the burial of knives and other kitchen objects in the earth in order to ritually cleanse (*kasher*) them. Christian tradition sees baptism in water as a spiritual transformation. Muslim, Bahá'í, Hindu, and Shinto traditions use water to ritually cleanse as well; Muslim tradition also permits using earth. Medicine people of North American tribes use sage smoke as well as sweat lodges as cleansing agents.

14. Mary Jo Heyen, interview by Rodger Kamenetz, The Shift Network's Dreamwork Summit (online conference), November 1, 2019.

15. Patricia Bulkley, "Invitation at the Threshold: Pre-Death Spiritual Experiences," in *Among All These Dreamers: Essays on Dreaming and Modern Society*, ed. Kelly Bulkeley (Albany, NY: State University of New York Press, 1996), 163–166.

16. Babylonian Talmud, Avodah Zarah 5b.

17. Jayne Gackenbach, "Reflections on Dreamwork with Central Alberta Cree: An Essay on an Unlikely Social Action Vehicle," in *Among All These Dreamers: Essays on Dreaming and Modern Society*, ed. Kelly Bulkeley (Albany, NY: State University of New York Press, 1996), 62–63.

18. Michael Meade, foreword to *Rites and Symbols of Initiation: The Mysteries of Birth and Rebirth*, by Mircea Eliade, trans. Willard R. Taske (Thompson, CT: Spring Publications, 1994), 8.

19. Babylonian Talmud, Berakhot 55b. The context of this prayer is that while the priestly blessing is recited in synagogue, the dreamer is simultaneously praying for the healing of a difficult or confusing dream. The transliteration of the Hebrew is: *Ribono shel Olam, ani shelakh vachalomotai shelakh. Chalom chalamti ve'ayni yodea mah hu. Im tovim hem—chazkeym ve'amtzeym kachalomotav shel Yosef. Ve'im tzrikhim refu'ah, refa'em keMiryam*

mitzaratah. Ken ḥafokhi kol chalomotai alai letovah.

If you would like a version in which the speaker, and God, are feminine, it would look like this: *Shekhinah, ani shelakh vachalomotai shelakh. Chalom chalamti ve'ayni yoda'at mah hu. Eem tovim hem—chazkeem ve'amtzeem kachalomotav shel Yosef. Ve'eem tzrikhim refu'ah, refa'eem keMiryam mitzaratah. Ken heefkhee kol chalo-motai alai letovah.*

שְׁכִינָה אֲנִי שֶׁלָךְ וַחֲלוֹמוֹתַי שֶׁלָךְ:
חֲלוֹם חָלַמְתִּי וְאֵינִי יוֹדַעַת מָה הוּא.
אִם טוֹבִים הֵם—חַזְקֵים וְאַמְּצִים
כַּחֲלוֹמוֹתָיו שֶׁל יוֹסֵף. וְאִם צְרִיכִים
רְפוּאָה—רְפָאִים כְּמִרְיָם מִצָּרַעְתָּהּ. כֵּן
הִפְכִי כָּל חֲלוֹמוֹתַי עָלַי לְטוֹבָה.

EPILOGUE: DREAMING THE CIRCLE
—
GUIDANCE FOR DREAM GROUPS

1. Taya Mâ Shere adapted LaKota OneHeart's ritual with her permission. At the time, LaKota OneHeart was using the name LaKotahasie Frazier.

2. Catherine Shainberg, *Kabbalah and the Power of Dreaming* (Rochester, VT: Inner Traditions, 2005); Robert Moss, *Conscious Dreaming: A Spiritual Path for Everyday Life* (New York: Three Rivers Press, 1996).

3. Babylonian Talmud, Berakhot 55b.

4. Babylonian Talmud, Berakhot 55b.

5. Taya Mâ believes she first heard this phrase from Eve Ilsen, a student and colleague of Madame Colette Aboulker-Muscat. Catherine Shainberg, a disciple and colleague of Madame Colette, uses the phrase "as a secondary dreamer of this dream." Both of these phrases suggest the dream interpreter, by envisioning the dream as the dreamer tells it, is also dreaming the dream.

6. Robert Moss, *Active Dreaming: Journeying Beyond Self-Limitation to a Life of Wild Dreaming* (Novato, CA: New World Library, 2011).

7. This is a way of testing an understanding of the dream that I also learned from Dr. Shainberg.

8. A Jewish movement founded by Rabbi Zalman Schachter-Shalomi and characterized by a liberal and mystical approach to Jewish life.

9. Zohar I, 200a.

10. From Kohenet Keshira haLev Fife.

11. Adapted from the traditional bedtime prayer. The Hebrew God-language is in the masculine. The transliteration of the text would be: *Makor Chayyim, tashkiveinu leshalom veta'amideinu leshalom utehei mitateinu shleimah*

lifanekha. Barukh atah, notein chalo-mot. If you would like to use feminine God-language in the prayer, it would read: *Makor Chayyim, tashkivinu leshalom veta'amidinu leshalom utehei mitateinu shleimah lifanayikh. Brukhah at, notenet chalomot.*

מְקוֹר חַיִּים תַּשְׁכִּיבֵנוּ לְשָׁלוֹם וְתַעֲמִידֵנוּ לְשָׁלוֹם וּתְהֵא מִטָּתֵינוּ שְׁלֵמָה לְפָנַיִךְ: בְּרוּכָה אַתְּ נוֹתֶנֶת חֲלוֹמוֹת.

12. From Joel Covitz, *Visions in the Night: Jungian and Ancient Dream Interpretation* (Scarborough, Ontario: Inner City Books, 2000), adapted from a dream incubation prayer in a Jewish mystical encyclopedia published in 1698. The transliteration of the text would be: *Makor Chayyim, Shekhinah kedoshah, pitchi lanu pitchei ma'alah u'fitchei meitah pitchei emet pitchei nevuah, halailah vehaleilot haba'im.* The Hebrew God-language is in the feminine.

13. Ana Sandoiu, "Why Do We Forget Our Dreams? Study Sheds Light," *Medical News Today*, September 23, 2019, https://www.medicalnewstoday.com/articles/326421.

References

Ada, a kohenet and chaplain, shared this dream with me. The dream shows her how to ground in her roots: the earth, her ancestors and tradition, her circle of friends. Tree roots provide nourishment and grounding: this is why we call our lineage our "roots." When we are in touch with our roots, we can know ourselves, find sustenance, and raise ourselves up. Ada climbs the mountain—we might call it Sinai, the mountain of revelation—assisted by her roots.

This reference section honors the roots of my dreamwork: teachers, colleagues, writers, poets, sages, mystics, dreamers, and researchers who have informed this book. The writings, texts, and interviews listed here have been essential to me in my dream explorations. I thank all the writers and speakers for their vision, their work, and their dedication. My journey, too, has been raised up by the roots beneath me.

Abram, David. *Becoming Animal: An Earthly Cosmology*. New York: Vintage Books, 2011.

Abram, David. "David Abram Interviewed by Derrick Jensen." Alliance for Wild Ethics. Accessed May 18, 2020. https://wildethics.org/essay/david-abram-interviewed-by-derrick-jensen.

Abram, David. *The Spell of the Sensuous: Perception and Language in a More-Than-Human World*. New York: Vintage Books, 1997.

Aizenstat, Stephen. *Dream Tending: Awakening to the Healing Power of Dreams*. New Orleans: Spring Journal, Inc., 2011.

"Anishinabe Dreams." *Native American Netroots*, September 25, 2010. http://nativeamericannetroots.net/diary/691.

Apps, Rozie. "Using Fungi to Clean Up Pollutants." *Permaculture Magazine*, February 5, 2015. https://www.permaculture.co.uk/readers-solutions/using-fungi-clean-pollutants.

Armistead, Samuel G., and Joseph H. Silverman. "A Judeo-Spanish Prayer." *La Corónica* 19, no.1 (1990–1991): 22–31.

Berry, Thomas. *The Dream of the Earth*. San Francisco: Sierra Club Books, 2006.

Binchy, D. A. "The Fair of Tailtiu and the Feast of Tara." *Ériu* 18 (1958): 113–138.

Bradbury, Ray. *Something Wicked This Way Comes*. New York: Simon & Schuster, 1997.

Bulkley, Patricia. "Invitation at the Threshold: Pre-Death Spiritual Experiences." In *Among All These Dreamers: Essays on Dreaming and Modern Society*, edited by Kelly Bulkeley. Albany, NY: State University of New York Press, 1996.

Byrne, F. J. *Irish Kings and High-Kings*. London: Batsford, 1973.

Caffrey, Margaret, and Patricia Francis, eds. *To Cherish the Life of the World: The Selected Letters of Margaret Mead*. New York: Basic Books, 2006.

Campbell, Joseph. *The Hero with a Thousand Faces*. Novato, CA: New World Library, 2008.

Casale, Alessandro. "Indigenous Dreams: Prophetic Nature, Spirituality, and Survivance." Indigenous New Hampshire Collaborative Collective. Accessed December 20, 2020. https://indigenousnh.com/2019/01/25/indigenous-dreams/.

Clark, Les, Eric Larson, and Wolfgang Reitherman, dirs. *Sleeping Beauty*. Walt Disney Productions, 1959.

Covitz, Joel. *Visions in the Night: Jungian and Ancient Dream Interpretation*. Scarborough, Ontario: Inner City Books, 2000.

Cummings, E. E. "maggie and milly and molly and may." In *Complete Poems: 1904–1962*, by E. E. Cummings. Edited by George J. Firmage. Revised edition. New York: Liveright Publishing Corporation, 2016.

Dashu, Max, dir. *Woman Shaman: The Ancients*. Collective Eye Films, 2013.

Duff, Kat. *The Secret Life of Sleep*. London: Oneworld, 2014.

Duffy, Connor. "Donald Trump Being Sued by Nine-Year-Old Levi Draheim Over His Climate Policies." ABC News, April 24, 2017. http://www.abc.net.au/news/2017-04-24/the-nine-year-old-suing-president-trump-over-his-climate-policy/8466946.

Dworschak, Manfred. "Europe Gone Wild: Back to Nature on the Continent." Translated by Christopher Sultan. *Spiegel Online*, October 24, 2013. https://www.spiegel.de/international/europe/rewilding-movement-seeks-to-return-areas-of-europe-to-wilderness-a-929573.html.

Eco, Umberto. *The Name of the Rose*. Translated by William Weaver. Boston: Mariner Books, 2014. First Italian publication in 1980 by Gruppo Editoriale. First English edition in 1983 by Harcourt, Inc.

Ehlert, Bette. "Healing Crimes: Dreaming Up the Solution to the Criminal Justice Mess." In *Among All These Dreamers: Essays on Dreaming and Modern Society*, edited by Kelly Bulkeley. Albany, NY: State University of New York Press, 1996.

Environmental Protection Agency (EPA). *EPA's 2008 Report on the Environment*. Washington, DC: National Center for

Environmental Assessment, 2008. https://cfpub.epa.gov/roe/documents/EPAROE_final_2008.pdf.

Fernandes, Marie. "The River as Metaphor." *Andrean Research Journal* 6 (2016–2017). https://standrewscollege.ac.in/wp-content/uploads/2018/06/The-River-as-Metaphor.pdf.

Firestone, Tirzah. *Wounds into Wisdom: Healing Intergenerational Jewish Trauma*. Rhinebeck, NY: Monkfish, 2019.

Fisher, Andy. *Radical Ecopsychology: Psychology in the Service of Life*. Albany, NY: State University of New York Press, 2002.

Gackenbach, Jayne. "Reflections on Dreamwork with Central Alberta Cree: An Essay on an Unlikely Social Action Vehicle." In *Among All These Dreamers: Essays on Dreaming and Modern Society*, edited by Kelly Bulkeley. Albany, NY: State University of New York Press, 1996.

Gackenbach, Jayne. "Research on Central Alberta Cree." Thoughts About Reflections on Dreamwork with Central Alberta Cree. Accessed November 11, 2017. http://www.sawka.com/spirit-watch/cresearc.htm.

Gaiman, Neil. *The Ocean at the End of the Lane*. New York: William Morrow, 2016.

Gates, Hill. "Money for the Gods." *Modern China* 13, no. 3 (July 1987): 259–277.

Gibbens, Sarah. "Scientists Are Trying to Save Coral Reefs. Here's What's Working." *National Geographic*, June 4, 2020. https://nationalgeographic.com/science/article/scientists-work-to-save-coral-reefs-climate-change-marine-parks.

Gillespie, Sally. "Climate Change and Psyche: Mapping Myths, Dreams and Conversations in the Era of Global Warming." PhD dissertation, Western Sydney University, 2014. http://researchdirect.uws.edu.au/islandora/object/uws%3A32281/datastream/PDF/view.

Ginzberg, Louis. *Legends of the Jews*. Philadelphia: Jewish Publication Society, 1938.

Glückel. *The Life of Glückel of Hameln: A Memoir*. Translated and edited by Beth-Zion Abrahams. Philadelphia: Jewish Publication Society, 2012.

Goldenberg, Naomi. "Dreams and Fantasies as Sources of Revelation: Feminist Appropriation of Jung." In *Womanspirit Rising: A Feminist Reader in Religion*, edited by Carol P. Christ and Judith Plaskow. San Francisco: HarperCollins, 1979.

Gordon, Hirsh Loeb. *The Maggid of Caro: The Mystic Life of the Eminent Codifier Joseph Caro as Revealed in His Secret Diary*. Whitefish, MT: Literary Licensing, 2013. First published in 1949.

Goulet, Jean-Guy A. "Dreams and Visions in Indigenous Lifeworlds: An Experiential Approach." *Canadian Journal of Native Studies* 13, no. 2 (1993): 171–198. http://www3.brandonu.ca/cjns/13.2/goulet.pdf.

Gujar, Ninad, Steven Andrew McDonald, Masaki Nishida, and Matthew P. Walker. "A Role for REM Sleep in Recalibrating the Sensitivity of the Human Brain to Specific Emotions." *Cerebral Cortex* 21 (January 2011): 115–123.

Hammer, Jill. *The Jewish Book of Days*. Philadelphia: Jewish Publication Society, 2006.

Hammer, Jill. *Return to the Place: The Magic, Meditation, and Mystery of Sefer Yetzirah*. Teaneck, NJ: Ben Yehuda Press, 2020.

Hammer, Jill, and Taya Shere. *The Hebrew Priestess: Ancient and New Visions of Jewish Women's Spiritual Leadership*. Teaneck, NJ: Ben Yehuda Press, 2015.

Harding, Stephan. *Animate Earth: Science, Intuition and Gaia*. White River Junction, VT: Chelsea Green Publishing Company, 2006.

Harding, Stephan. "Earth System Science and Gaian Science." Accessed November 11, 2017. https://is.muni.cz/el/1423/podzim2010/ENS244/um/Earth_System_Science_and_Gaian_Science.pdf.

Harvell, Drew. *A Sea of Glass: Searching for the Blaschkas' Fragile Legacy in an Ocean at Risk*. Oakland, CA: University of California Press, 2016.

Hearn, Lian. *Emperor of the Eight Islands: The Tale of Shikanoko, Book I*. New York: Farrar, Strauss, and Giroux, 2016.

Heyen, Mary Jo. *Dreaming into the Mystery: Exploring the Dreams and Visions of the Dying*. Davey Press, 2020.

Hillman, James. *The Dream and the Underworld*. New York: Harper and Row, 1979.

Hoel, Erik. "The Overfitted Brain: Dreams Evolved to Assist Generalization." *Patterns* 2, no. 5 (May 2021): 1–15. https://doi.org/10.1016/j.patter.2021.100244.

Hur, Nam-lin. *Prayer and Play in Late Tokugawa Japan: Asakusa Sensōji and Edo Society*. Cambridge, MA: Harvard University Press, 2000.

Institut de Recherche pour le Développement (IRD). "Mangroves: A Filter for Heavy Metals." *ScienceDaily*, July 24, 2012. https.// www.sciencedaily.com/releases/2012/07/120724104304.htm.

Jaenke, Karen. "Dreaming with the Ancestors." *ReVision* 28, no. 4 (Spring 2006): 28–35.

Jensen, Derrick. *Dreams*. New York: Seven Stories Press, 2011.

Jewish Publication Society, The. *JPS Hebrew-English Tanakh*. Philadelphia: Jewish Publication Society, 1999.

Johnson, Cait. *Earth, Water, Fire, and Air: Essential Ways of Connecting to Spirit*. Nashville, TN: Skylight Paths, 2002.

Judson, Katharine Berry. *Myths and Legends of the Great Plains*. Charleston, SC: BiblioBazaar, 2008.

Jung, C. G. *The Archetypes and the Collective Unconscious: The Collected Works of C. G. Jung*, Volume 9 (Part I). Edited and translated by Gerhard Adler and R. F. C. Hull. Princeton, NJ: Princeton University Press, 1968.

Jung, C. G. *The Earth Has a Soul: C. G. Jung on Nature, Technology, and Modern Life*. Edited by Meredith Sabini. Berkeley, CA: North Atlantic Books, 2002.

Jung, C. G. "The Meaning of Psychology for Modern Man" (1933). In *Civilization in Transition: The Collected Works of C. G. Jung*, Volume 10, edited and translated by Gerhard Adler and R. F. C. Hull. Princeton, NJ: Princeton University Press, 1970.

Jung, C. G. *Mysterium Coniunctionis: The Collected Works of C. G. Jung*, Volume 14. Edited and translated by Gerhard Adler and R. F. C. Hull. Princeton, NJ: Princeton University Press, 1977.

Kallet, Cindy. *Working on Wings to Fly*. Folk-Legacy Records, 1981.

Kamenetz, Rodger. *The History of Last Night's Dream: Discovering the Hidden Path to the Soul*. New York: HarperOne, 2007.

Kamenetz, Rodger. "The Poetic Imagination and the Natural Dream." Natural Dreamwork, April 9, 2021. https://www.the-naturaldream.com/dream-poetry/.

Kamenetz, Rodger. "The Sacred Encounter in Our Dreams." Natural Dreamwork and the Sacred Encounter. Class for The Shift Network, December 12, 2019. https://theshiftnetwork.com/course/NaturalDreamwork.

Kellaway, Kate. "When We Dream, We Have the Perfect Chemical Canvas for Intense Visions." *The Guardian*, April 14, 2019. https://www.theguardian.com/science/2019/apr/14/dreams-perfect-canvas-intense-visions-alice-robb-interview.

King, Leonard W. *Enuma Elish: The Seven Tablets of Creation; The Babylonian and Assyrian Legends Concerning the Creation of the World and Mankind*. New York: Cosimo Classics, 2010. First published in 1902.

Kline, Dana L. *Contextualizing Transformation: Initiation Dreams of Depth Psychotherapists-in-Training*. Master's Thesis, Pacifica Graduate Institute, 2014. https://core.ac.uk/display/323411503.

Larrington, Carolyne, trans. *The Poetic Edda*. Oxford: Oxford University Press, 1996.

Le Guin, Ursula K. *A Wizard of Earthsea*. Boston: Houghton Mifflin, 1968.

L'Engle, Madeleine. *A Wrinkle in Time*. New York: Square Fish Books, 2007.

Lennox, Michael. *Dream Sight: A Dictionary and Guide for Interpreting Any Dream*. Woodbury, MN: Llewellyn Publications, 2011.

Li, Qing. *Forest Bathing: How Trees Can Help Us Find Health and Happiness*. New York: Viking, 2018.

Maathai, Wangari. "Nobel Lecture." The Nobel Prize, December 10, 2004. https://nobelprize.org/prizes/peace/2004/maathai/26050-wangari-maathai-nobel-lecture-2004/.

Mahadevan, Priya, and Virginia Prescott. "Nightmares and Viral Scares: How COVID-19 Manifests in Our Dreams." Georgia Public Broadcasting, May 8, 2020. Updated August 13, 2020. https://www.gpb.org/news/2020/05/08/nightmares-and-viral-scares-how-covid-19-manifests-in-our-dreams.

Makin, Simon. "Deep Sleep Gives Your Brain a Deep Clean." *Scientific American*, November 1, 2019. https://scientificamerican.com/article/deep-sleep-gives-your-brain-a-deep-clean1/.

Masterman, E. W. G. "Jewish Customs of Birth, Marriage, and Death." *The Biblical World* 22, no. 4 (1903): 248–257.

Matt, Daniel. *The Zohar: Pritzker Edition*. Stanford, CA: Stanford University Press, 2003.

McCone, Kim. *Pagan Past and Christian Present in Early Irish Literature*. Maynooth, Ireland: Maynooth Monographs, 1990.

Meade, Michael. Foreword to *Rites and Symbols of Initiation: The Mysteries of Birth and Rebirth*, by Mircea Eliade. Translated by Willard R. Taske. Thompson, CT: Spring Publications, 1994.

Mikaelson, Ben. *Touching Spirit Bear*. New York: HarperCollins, 2002.

Mistele, William R. *Undines: Lessons from the Realm of the Water Spirits*. Berkeley, CA: North Atlantic Books, 2010.

Miyazaki, Hayao, dir. *Castle in the Sky*. Tokyo: Studio Ghibli, 2003.

Monaghan, Patricia. *The Goddess Path: Myths, Invocations, and Rituals*. Woodbury, MN: Llewellyn Publications, 1999.

Monaghan, Patricia. "Harvest Evening." In *Grace of Ancient Land*. New Orleans: Voices from the American Land, 2011. http://www.voicesfromtheamericanland.org/html/monaghan.html.

Morrison, Toni. *Song of Solomon*. New York: Vintage International, 2004.

Moss, Robert. *Active Dreaming: Journeying Beyond Self-Limitation to a Life of Wild Freedom*. Novato, CA: New World Library, 2011.

Moss, Robert. *Conscious Dreaming: A Spiritual Path for Everyday Life*. New York: Three Rivers Press, 1996.

Myers, Brynn. *The Echoed Life of Jorja Graham*. 2nd edition. Florida: Indigo Ink Publications, 2021.

Nielsen, Ivar. "Spiritual Visions." Accessed November 11, 2017. http://www.native-science.net/Visions.Dreams.htm.

Novick, Leah. "Shekhinah Theology of the Future." *Delumin/a*, March 15, 2015. http://delumina.net/blog/tag/Leah+Novick.

Ochs, Vanessa. *The Jewish Dream Book: The Key to Opening the Inner Meaning of Your Dreams*. Woodstock, VT: Jewish Lights, 2003.

Oliver, Mary. "The Summer Day." In *New and Selected Poems*. Boston: Beacon Press, 1992.

Ostriker, Alicia. *The Volcano Sequence*. Pittsburgh: University of Pittsburgh Press, 2002.

Paracelsus. *The Hermetic and Alchemical Writings of Paracelsus*. Edited by Arthur Edward Waite. Eastford, CT: Martino Fine Books, 2009.

Pathak, Prateek. "Why Lord Krishna Is Known as 'Banke Bihari.'" *The Speaking Tree*, March 23, 2015. https://www.speaking-tree.in/allslides/why-lord-krishna-is-known-as-banke-bihari.

Petty, Jules. *The Earth Only Endures: On Reconnecting with Nature and Our Place in It*. New York: Earthscan, 2007.

Pitzele, Peter. *Scripture Windows: Toward a Practice of Bibliodrama*. Los Angeles: Torah Aura Productions, 1998.

Pongratz-Leisten, Beate. "Sacred Marriages and the Transfer of Divine Knowledge: Alliances between the Gods and the King in Ancient Mesopotamia." In *Sacred Marriages: The Divine-Human Sexual Metaphor from Sumer to Early Christianity,* edited by Martti Nissinen and Risto Uro. Winona Lake, IN: Eisenbrauns, 2008.

Popova, Maria. "How Mendeleev Invented His Periodic Table in a Dream." *Brain Pickings,* February 8, 2016. https://www.brainpickings.org/2016/02/08/mendeleev -periodic-table-dream/.

Popova, Maria. "Life Is Like Blue Jelly: Margaret Mead Discovers the Meaning of Existence in a Dream." *Brain Pickings,* February 25, 2014. https://www.brainpickings.org/2014/02/25/margaret -mead-meaning-of-life/.

Pugh, Thomas A. M., Mats Lindeskog, Benjamin Smith, Benjamin Poulter, Almut Arneth, Vanessa Haverd, and Leonardo Calle. "Role of Forest Regrowth in Global Carbon Sink Dynamics." *Proceedings of the National Academy of Sciences of the United States of America* 116, no. 10 (2019): 4382–4387. https://doi. org/10.1073/pnas.1810512116.

Ravenhill, Philip. *Dreams and Reverie: Images of Otherworld Mates Among the Baule, West Africa.* Washington, DC: Smithsonian Institution Press, 1996.

Rich, Adrienne. "Quarto." In *Tonight No Poetry Will Serve: Poems 2007–2010.* New York: W. W. Norton & Company, 2011.

Rilke, Rainer Maria. "How Surely Gravity's Law." In *Rilke's Book of Hours: Love Poems to God,* edited by Anita Barrows and Joanna Macy. New York: Riverhead Books, 1997.

Rimbaud, Arthur. *A Season in Hell and the Drunken Boat/Une Saison en Enfer et Le Bateau Ivre.* Translated by Louise Varèse. New York: New Directions, 1961. First published in 1873.

Rubin, Jessica A., and J. H. Görres. "Potential for Mycorrhizae-Assisted Phytoremediation of Phosphorus for Improved Water Quality." *International Journal of Environmental Research and Public Health* 18, no. 1 (January 2021). https://doi.org/ 10.3390/ijerph18010007.

Rukeyser, Muriel. "Akiba." In *The Collected Poems of Muriel Rukeyser*, edited by Janet E. Kaufman and Anne F. Herzog. Pittsburgh: University of Pittsburgh Press, 2005.

Sabini, Meredith. "Dreaming a New Paradigm." In *Ecotherapy: Healing with Nature in Mind*, edited by Linda Buzzell and Craig Chalquist. Berkeley, CA: Counterpoint, 2009.

Sabini, Meredith. "Dreaming for Our Survival." *Depth Insights*, Fall 2013. http://www.depthinsights.com/Depth-Insights-scholarly-ezine/e-zine-issue-5-fall-2013/dreaming-for-our-survival-by-meredith-sabini/.

Sandoiu, Ana. "Why Do We Forget Our Dreams? Study Sheds Light." *Medical News Today*, September 23, 2019. https://www.medicalnewstoday.com/articles/326421.

Schachter-Shalomi, Zalman. "The Spirituality of the Future: Toward a New and Kerygmatic Credo." The Shalom Center, May 9, 2008. https://theshalomcenter.org/node/1395.

Schiller, Rivka. "'Psychic Dreams,' Witches, Curses, and Other Family Secrets." Rivka's Yiddish, June 25, 2017. http://www.rivkasyiddish.com/blog/psychic-dreams-witches-curses-and-other-family-secrets.

Schilling, LaChelle. "Desierto Divino: Messages from the Earth." *Feminism and Religion*, February 17, 2017. https://feminismandreligion.com/2017/02/17/desierto-divino-messages-from-the-earth-by-lachelle-schilling/.

Schroeder, Herbert. "Seeking the Balance: Do Dreams Have a Role in Natural Resource Management?" In *Among All These Dreamers: Essays on Dreaming and Modern Society*, edited by Kelly Bulkeley. Albany, NY: State University of New York Press, 1996.

Schwartz, Howard. *Tree of Souls: The Mythology of Judaism*. Oxford: Oxford University Press, 2007.

Seidenberg, David. *Kabbalah and Ecology: God's Image in the More-Than-Human World*. Cambridge: Cambridge University Press, 2016.

Sered, Susan. *Women as Ritual Experts: The Religious Lives of Elderly Jewish Women in Jerusalem*. Oxford: Oxford University Press, 1992.

Shafton, Anthony. *Dream-Singers: The African American Way with Dreams*. Hoboken, NJ: John Wiley and Sons, 2002.

Shainberg, Catherine. *DreamBirth: Transforming the Journey of Childbirth through Dreaming*. Louisville, CO: SoundsTrue, 2014.

Shainberg, Catherine. "The Hidden Treasures of Dreaming." *Spirit of Ma'at*. https://www.yumpu.com/en/document/view/50861966/the-hidden-treasures-of-dreaming-spirit-of-maat.

Shainberg, Catherine. *Kabbalah and the Power of Dreaming*. Rochester, VT: Inner Traditions, 2005.

Shainberg, Catherine. Quoted in "We Are Always Dreaming." Interview by Tami Simon. *Insights at the Edge,* Sounds True, January 21, 2014. https://www.resources.soundstrue.com/podcast/we-are-always-dreaming/.

Sharp, Jonathan. *Divining Your Dreams: How the Ancient Mystical Tradition of the Kabbalah Can Help You Interpret 1,000 Dream Images*. New York: Atria Books, 2002.

Shift Network, The. Dreamwork Summit (online dream conference hosted by Rodger Kamenetz and Kezia Vida). October 29–November 1, 2019. https://support.theshiftnetwork.com/hc/en-us/articles/360038027013-Dreamwork-Summit-2019.

Shiva, Vandana, and Maria Mies. *Ecofeminism*. London: Zed Books, 2014.

Shlain, Leonard. *The Alphabet Versus the Goddess: The Conflict Between Word and Image*. New York: Penguin Compass, 1999.

Siderius, Edmund. "Knowledge in Nature, Knowledge of Nature: Paracelsus and the Elementals." The Starry Messenger, March 8, 2011. https://edmundsiderius.wordpress.com/2011/03/08/knowledge-in-nature-knowledge-of-nature-paracelsus-and-the-elementals/.

Smith, C. M. *Jung and Shamanism in Dialogue: Retrieving the Soul/Retrieving the Sacred*. Mahwah, NJ: Paulist Press, 1997.

Sohei, Dare. "Musings from a Transformed Being." Think Movement, September 6, 2020. https://thinkmovement. net/2020/09/06/musings-from-a-transformed-being/.

Sohn, Ruth. "I Shall Sing to the Lord a New Song." In *Kol Haneshamah: Shabbat Vehagim, Reconstructionist Prayerbook*. Wyncote, PA: Reconstructionist Press, 1989.

Somé, Malidoma Patrice. *The Healing Wisdom of Africa: Finding Life Purpose through Nature, Ritual, and Community*. New York: TarcherPerigee, 1999.

Starhawk. "Lessons from the Fires." Accessed November 11, 2017. http://starhawk.org/lessons-from-the-fires/.

Steinbeck, John. *The Log from the Sea of Cortez*. New York: Penguin Books, 1951.

Steinsaltz, Adin. *The Thirteen Petalled Rose: A Discourse on the Essence of Jewish Existence and Belief*. New York: Basic Books, 2006.

Toko-pa. "Dreamspeak: Ancestral Healing." May 28, 2013. https:// toko-pa.com/2013/05/28/dreamspeak-ancestral-healing/.

Van den Daele, Leland. "Direct Interpretation of Dreams: Neuropsychology." *American Journal of Psychoanalysis* 56 (1996): 253–268.

Vital, Hayyim. "Book of Visions." In *Jewish Mystical Autobiographies: Book of Visions and Book of Secrets*, edited and translated by Morris M. Faierstein. Mahwah, NJ: Paulist Press, 1999.

Wallace, Marion. "'Making Tradition': Healing, History and Ethnic Identity among Otjiherero-Speakers in Namibia, c. 1850–1950." *Journal of Southern African Studies* 29, no. 2 (June 2003): 355–372. https://doi.org/10.1080/03057070306212.

Weaver, Natalie. "In Dreams." *Feminism and Religion*, October 2, 2019. https://feminismandreligion.com/2019/10/02/in-dreams -by-natalie-weaver/.

Weissler, Chava. *Voices of the Matriarchs: Listening to the Prayers of Early Modern Jewish Women*. Boston: Beacon Press, 1998.

Wezerek, Gus, and Nicholas Konrad. "20 Dreams from 2020." *New York Times*, June 12, 2020. https://www.nytimes.com/interactive/2020/06/12/opinion/reader-dreams-2020.html.

Wiener, Shohama. "Rosh Hashanah 2009/5770: A Ladder to Heaven." Temple Beth-El of City Island, August 31, 2009. https://yourshulbythesea.org/2009/08/31/rosh-hashanah-20095770/.

Wilson, Matthew. "Animals Have Complex Dreams, MIT Researcher Proves." *MIT News*, January 24, 2001. http://news.mit.edu/2001/dreaming.

Wolkstein, Diane, and Samuel Noah Kramer. *Inanna, Queen of Heaven and Earth: Her Stories and Hymns from Sumer*. San Francisco: HarperPerennial, 1983.

Yassif, Eli. *The Legend of Safed: Life and Fantasy in the City of Kabbalah*. Translated by Haim Watzman. Detroit: Wayne State University Press, 2019.

Yupanqui, Tika (Tracy Marks). "The Iroquois Dream Experience and Spirituality, Part One." WebWinds, 1988. http://www.web-winds.com/yupanqui/iroquoisdreams.htm.

Zelda. "Moon is Teaching Bible." In *The Book of Blessings: New Jewish Prayers for Daily Life, the Sabbath, and the New Moon Festival*, by Marcia Falk. Boston: Beacon Press, 1999.

Znamenski, Andrei A., ed. *Shamanism: Critical Concepts in Sociology*. London and New York: RoutledgeCurzon, 2004.

Zornberg, Avivah Gottlieb. *Moses: A Human Life*. New Haven, CT: Yale University Press, 2016.

Zornberg, Avivah Gottlieb. *The Murmuring Deep: Reflections on the Biblical Unconscious*. New York: Schocken Books, 2009.

Zumwait, Rosemary Lévy. "Las Buenas Mujeres: The Keepers of Sephardic Health and Home." *Jewish Folklore and Etymology Review* 15, no. 2 (1993): 107–112.

Bible (8th–1st century CE)

Babylonian Talmud (5th–6th century CE)

Midrash Tanhuma (midrash, 9th century CE)

Likutei Moharan (Nachman of Breslov, 18th–19th century CE)

Likutei Tefillot (Nachman of Breslov, 18th–19th century CE)

Otzar haMidrashim (midrash, 5th–13th century CE)

Pirkei Avot (2nd–3rd century CE)

Sha'arei Kedushah (Hayyim Vital, 16th century CE)

Sha'arei Orah (Yosef Ibn Gikatilla, 13th century CE)

Sifrei (midrash, 3rd century CE)

Yalkut Bereishit (midrash, 13th century CE)

Zohar (13th century CE)

The Bible translation is the author's or comes from the *JPS Hebrew-English Tanakh* (Philadelphia: Jewish Publication Society, 1999). Other translations are the author's or come from sefaria.org.

Rabbi Jill Hammer, PhD, is an author, scholar, ritualist, poet, midrashist, and dreamworker. She is the Director of Spiritual Education at the Academy for Jewish Religion, a pluralistic seminary, and cofounder of the Kohenet Hebrew Priestess Institute, a program in earth-based, embodied, feminist Jewish spiritual leadership. Her other works include *Return to the Place: The Magic, Meditation, and Mystery of Sefer Yetzirah; The Hebrew Priestess: Ancient and New Visions of Jewish Women's Spiritual Leadership* (with Taya Shere); *The Jewish Book of Days: A Companion for All Seasons; Sisters at Sinai: New Tales of Biblical Women;* and *The Book of Earth and Other Mysteries.* She and her family live in Manhattan.

Ayin Press is an artist-run publishing platform, production studio, and research collective rooted in Jewish culture and emanating outward. We create and support work at the intersection of Political Imagination, Speculative Theology, and Radical Aesthetics.

Ayin's Speculative Theology series publishes work that springs from the depths and margins of human spirituality. Whether emerging from within a particular wisdom tradition or dreaming beyond its current borders, each text is a testament to the impossible art of naming what cannot be fully named: experiences of the divine, the hidden, the infinite. We curate works committed to reimagining ritual, prayer, hermeneutics, mitzvot; to wrestling with faith and its absence; to seeding many possible spiritual futures.

Ayin Press was founded on a deep belief in the power of culture and creativity to heal, transform, and uplift the world we share and build together. We are committed to amplifying a polyphony of voices from within and beyond the Jewish world.

For more information about our current or upcoming projects and titles, reach out to us at info@ayinpress.org. To make a tax-deductible contribution to our work, visit our website at www.ayinpress.org/donate.